Charlotte Keat

Our Father

Published by Methuen Drama 2012

Methuen Drama, an imprint of Bloomsbury Publishing Plc

1 3 5 7 9 10 8 6 4 2

Methuen Drama
Bloomsbury Publishing Plc
50 Bedford Square
London WC1B 3DP
www.methuendrama.com

ISBN 978 1 408 17251 3

A CIP record for this book is available from the British Library

Available in the USA from Bloomsbury Academic & Professional, 175 Fifth
Avenue /3rd Floor, New York, NY 10010. www.BloomsburyAcademicUSA.com

Typeset by Mark Heslington Ltd, Scarborough, North Yorkshire
Printed and bound in Great Britain by CPI Group (UK) Ltd, Croydon, CR0 4YY

OUR FATHER
by Charlotte Keatley

Commissioned by and first performed at Watford Palace Theatre from 17 February to 3 March 2012

Cast (in order of appearance)

2012

Anna (born 1982)	Anna O'Grady
Jack (born 1979)	Chris Kelham
Bill (Anna's father, born 1945)	Paul Greenwood
Sheila (Anna's mother, born 1950)	Julia St John

1212

Catherine (an anchoress)	Faye Winter
Priest	Chris Kelham

Creative Team

Director	Brigid Larmour
Designer	Adam Wiltshire
Movement Director	Shona Morris
Lighting Designer	Jenny Cane
Sound Designer	Rich Walsh
Casting Director	Kay Magson CDG
Deputy Stage Manager	Maddie Baylis
Assistant Stage Manager	Ian Grigson

Thanks to Lawrence Osborn, Kate Flatt

Website: www.ourfatherplay.com

Scenes

Location

The play takes place around a huge reservoir surrounded by hills in the Peak district of the north of England.

ACT ONE

ACT TWO

Cast Biographies

Anna O'Grady Anna

Watford Palace Theatre: Kate in Family Business (2011), Stephanie in Time of My Life (2011).

Anna graduated from LAMDA in the summer of 2009. Theatre includes Birthday Letters (RSC – Workshop). Her film and television credits include Black Pond and Holby City.

Chris Kelham Jack/Priest

Watford Palace Theatre: Family Business (2011), Time of My Life (2011), The Dresser (2008).

Chris trained at the Guildford School of Acting and was a recipient of the Carleton Hobbs BBC Radio Drama Award. Since then he has appeared in numerous radio plays for the BBC, including six series as Howard in Ladies of Letters for BBC Radio 4, Toby in Amy's View (original West End cast), Romeo in Romeo and Juliet (National Audio Drama Award), Wuthering Heights and several Woman's Hour readings. Audio Books include Shatter, David Mitchell's No.9 Dream and Ghostwritten. His theatre credits include Brecht – Poetry and Song (King's Place, London), Another Country (Arts Theatre), Paresis (Bristol Old Vic), Scenes from an Execution (Hackney Empire), Ignatius Trail (Lyric Hammersmith/ Royal Exchange, Manchester), A Christmas Carol (National reading tour). His television credits include Hustle, Trial and Retribution, Last Voices of a Generation for the BBC. Films include The Cost of Love, Over the Edge, What's Your Name 41. Chris has also appeared in numerous readings with Actors for Human Rights.

Faye Winter Catherine

Theatre includes: Comedy of Errors (Regent's Park Open Air Theatre), Hamlet (Donmar at Wyndhams and Broadway), Country Wife (Theatre Royal Haymarket), The Beggar's Opera (Gilt & Grime), Hung Up (Pact Imagination), Uncommon Women & Others (New Players Theatre). Television includes: Doctors (BBC). Film: Losing Innocence (Pretty Hate Productions).

Julia St John Sheila

Julia trained at LAMDA. Theatre includes seasons
with Common Stock Theatre Company, Theatr Clwyd,
New Victoria Theatre Newcastle Under Lyme,
Larkrise (Almeida Theatre), Nana for Shared
Experience (Almeida Theatre), A Tale of Two Cities
(Cambridge Theatre Company), The Three Sisters
(Chichester Festival Theatre), The Madness of George
III (West Yorkshire Playhouse and Birmingham Rep),
The Archbishop's Ceiling (Southwark Playhouse). TV includes The
Brittas Empire, GBH, A Question of Attribution, The Grand, The
Victoria Wood Show, Gone to the Dogs, The Glass, Harry Enfield and
Chums, The Blackheath Poisonings, Poirot, Julian Fellowes' Most
Mysterious Murders, A Place of Execution, A Touch of Frost, Lewis,
Casualty. Film includes The Young Victoria.

Paul Greenwood Bill

Theatre: most recently The Rivals, Proof and The
Admiral Crichton (The New Vic Theatre), Bomber's
Moon (Coventry Belgrade). Other credits include
Malvolio in Twelfth Night (The Ludlow Festival),
Polonius in Hamlet (The Haymarket, Basingstoke),
Norman in The Norman Conquests, Fancourt Babberly
in Charley's Aunt, Terry Dennis in Privates on Parade,
Victor in The Price, Moon in The Real Inspector Hound,
and Harold in Black Comedy. London Theatre: Twelfth Night and
Inadmissible Evidence (Royal Court). Piaf and Once in a Lifetime
(RSC). UK Tours: Sky in Guys and Dolls. Recently he toured in The
Shakespeare Revue and played The Grandfather in Chitty Chitty
Bang Bang. Royal Shakespeare Company: Antipholus of Syracuse
in The Comedy of Errors, Polixenes in The Winter's Tale, Lysander
in A Midsummer Night's Dream, Robert in They Shoot Horses,
Don't They?, Kent in King Lear, Hank/The Scarecrow in The Wizard
of Oz, Bob Cratchit in A Christmas Carol, Feste in Twelfth Night
and Buckingham in Henry VIII. Television: title role in Rosie. Also
appeared in Coronation Street, A Day Out, The Growing Pains of
Adrian Mole, Spender, Heartbeat, Holby City, Doctors, Casualty,
Midsomer Murders. Radio: Wives and Daughters.

Creative Team Biographies

Charlotte Keatley Writer

Charlotte started by acting, writing, directing and making the set for: Underneath the Arndale (Contact Theatre, foyer) in 1981, The Iron Serpent (Leeds Theatre Workshop) in 1983; An Armenian Childhood (Leeds) in 1983 with Impact Theatre; The Legend Of Padgate (community play in 1985). Subsequent plays include: Waiting for Martin (English Shakespeare Company) in 1987; My Mother Said I Never Should (Contact Theatre, Manchester) 1987 (directed by Brigid Larmour), and Royal Court in 1989 – since translated into 23 languages, a set text in schools and universities, named by the National Theatre in 2000 as one of the Significant Plays of the Twentieth Century; Fears and Miseries in the Third Term – co-writer (Young Vic) in 1989; The Singing Ringing Tree (Contact Theatre) in 1992; The Sleep of Reason Produces Monsters (Leeds Theatre Workshop and Shanghai Academy Theatre) in 1999. For schools: Forest premiered at St Wilfred's School, Blackburn in 2001; The First Pirate Queen premiered at WGS school Manchester in 2005. Unproduced as yet: All the Daughters of War commissioned by the RSC, workshops at RADA in 2007 and National Theatre Studio in 2008. Our Father was commissioned by Watford Palace Theatre where Charlotte Keatley is a Creative Associate. Awards include George Devine Award, Manchester Evening News Best New Play, nominated for Olivier Award – Most Promising Newcomer, Time Out Theatre Award, Edinburgh Fringe First, Sunday Times Outstanding Performance Award. She has written numerous dramas for BBC Radio 4, a children's drama Badger for Granada TV and a film script Falling Slowly for Channel 4. As an arts journalist she has written for the Observer, Financial Times, Yorkshire Post, Scotsman, Performance Magazine and contributed live on BBC radio and television arts programmes for many years. For the Guardian she has written on the Rose Revolution in Georgia, having travelled extensively in Georgia and Abkhazia, about which she is writing a book. Charlotte researched and filmed in children's prisons in Georgia for the Channel 4 documentary Kids Behind Bars (2003), for which the research team won an Emmy Award. She has taught creative writing from Burnley to Shanghai and continues to run workshops in schools, universities and for community groups of all ages. She lives with her daughter Georgia, in Manchester, and goes rock-climbing instead of cleaning the house.

Brigid Larmour Director

Brigid Larmour is Artistic Director and Chief Executive of Watford Palace Theatre. She has directed for the Palace: Alan Ayckbourn's Time of My Life and Absent Friends, Gary Owen's We That are Left and Mrs Reynolds and the Ruffian, Shakespeare's As You Like It, Charlotte Keatley's My Mother Said I Never Should and Von Ribbentrop's Watch by Laurence Marks and Maurice Gran (a co-production with Oxford Playhouse).

Brigid is a producer, director, dramaturg and teacher with experience in the subsidised and commercial theatre and television. From 1998 to 2006 she was Artistic Director of West End company Act Productions, and adviser to BBC4 Plays. From 1993 to 1998 she directed a series of promenade Shakespeares, Shakespeare Unplugged, for RNT Education. From 1989 to 1994 she was Artistic Director of Contact Theatre, Manchester, commissioning the first British plays responding to the rave scene (Excess/XS), and the implications of virtual reality (Strange Attractors, a multimedia promenade production), both by Manchester poet Kevin Fegan. She trained at the RSC, and as a studio director at Granada TV.

Adam Wiltshire Designer

Trained in theatre design at the Royal Welsh College of Music and Drama, he became a group winner of the Linbury Biennial for Theatre Design in 2003. Theatre productions include My Mother Said I Never Should (West Yorkshire Playhouse), Much Ado About Nothing (Salisbury Playhouse), David Copperfield (Mercury Theatre) and shows for Unicorn Theatre, Oval Playhouse, New Wolsey Theatre and the Guildhall School of Music and Drama. Opera designs include Roméo et Juliette and Duke Bluebeard's Castle (Opera North), Teseo, Katya Kabanova, Promised End (English Touring Opera) and operas for Almedia Opera, The Opera Group and Royal Northern College of Music. Ballet credits for the Royal Ballet include: Being and Having Been, Tanglewood, Childen of Adam and Sensorium (Royal Opera House main stage). Adam is currently working on productions for the Royal College of Music and a Tamasha/Circus space collaboration.

Shona Morris Movement Director

Watford Palace Theatre: My Mother Said I Never Should, As You Like It, The Dresser, An English Tragedy and Lysistrata.

For the Stratford Festival Theatre in Canada, where she regularly works as a movement coach with the company, movement directing credits include: Peter Pan, The Winter's Tale, Dangerous Liaisons, King Lear, Henry VIII, Agamemnon, Electra, The Flies, The Birds and Julius Caesar. For the Chichester Festival Theatre: Twelfth Night and Nicholas Nickleby (tour and West End). For the National Theatre Studio, Swine (directed) and Early Morning and Stallerhoff (directed). Also I Caught Crabs in Walberswick (Eastern Angles/Edinburgh Festival/Bush), Invasion (Soho Theatre), Snow Spider (Tristan Bates Theatre), Atman (The Latchmere), The Tempest (Liverpool Playhouse), Oedipus Rex (Cambridge Arts Theatre). She works for the Vienna Kinder Theatre. Acting credits include (recently) Sarah Kahn in Chicken Soup with Barley at the Nottingham Playhouse and Tricycle Theatre. Shona is currently Course Leader of the BA Acting Course at Drama Centre, where she teaches mask, movement and chorus work.

Jenny Cane Lighting Designer

Jenny has designed theatre, opera, musical and dance productions in the West End and throughout Britain as well as in Europe, North America and Australia. Her work in regional repertory theatre in Britain is extensive and includes productions at Haymarket Leicester where she has lit over 30 productions. Many of her productions have been seen in the West End. These include Cafe Puccini, Requiem, Variations, Eurovision, Follies, Nine and Sweeney Todd at the Royal Festival Hall; drama productions in London include Welcome to Ramallah (Arcola, 2008), Chapter II, The Aspern Papers, The Odd Couple and Three Tall Women.

In 2010 she lit A Little Night Music at the Théâtre du Châtelet, Paris. Her lighting designs for Eugene Onegin continue in repertoire at the English National Opera and she worked on many productions there including Der Rosenkavalier, Falstaff, Madam

Butterfly, Peter Grimes and The Barber of Seville. She designed the lighting for The Magic Flute in Antwerp and more recently Die Fledermaus for Scottish Opera Go Round and The Turn of the Screw in Macedonia. She returned to Scottish Opera in 2008 for the highly praised A Night at the Chinese Opera and in 2010 she lit Orfeo Ed Euridice for Minnesota Opera.

Rich Walsh Sound Designer

Previous sound designs include: Travelling Light, Welcome to Thebes, The Observer, Baby Girl, DNA, The Miracle, The Five Wives of Maurice Pinder, Landscape with Weapon, The Reporter, The Alchemist, Exiles, Southwark Fair, The Mandate, Primo, The False Servant, Sing Yer Heart Out for the Lads, Scenes from The Big Picture, Dinner, Closing Time, The Associate, Sanctuary, The Mentalists, The Shadow of a Boy, Free, The Walls (National Theatre); Exposure, Under the Blue Sky, On Raftery's Hill, Sacred Heart, Trust, Choice (Royal Court); Primo (Broadway); Vernon God Little (Young Vic); Dinner (Wyndhams); What the Night is For (Comedy); 50 Revolutions (Whitehall); Time of My Life (Watford Palace Theatre); The Price (Tricycle Theatre); How to be an Other Woman (Gate Theatre); Eigengrau (Bush Theatre); The Stock Da'wa (Hampstead Downstairs); Strike Gently Away from Body (Young Vic Studio); Small Craft Warnings (The Pleasance); Dirk (The Oxford Playhouse); Von Ribbentrop's Watch, Rock, Fimbles Live!, The Lady in the Van, The Deep Blue Sea, The Unexpected Man, The Nation's Favourite – The True Adventures of Radio One (National Tours). Associate Sound Designer on: Beauty and the Beast, The Cat in the Hat (National Theatre); An Anatomie in Four Quarters (Sadler's Wells); and Cool Hand Luke (Aldwych Theatre).

Kay Magson CDG Casting Director

Theatre credits include: The Solid Gold Cadillac (Garrick); Dangerous Corner (West Yorkshire Playhouse/West End); Round the Horne Revisited, Dracula (National tours); Singin' in the Rain (West Yorkshire Playhouse, National Theatre/National tour); Aspects of Love, All the Fun of the Fair and The Witches of Eastwick (National tours); Kes (Liverpool and National tour);

Great Expectations (Watford Palace Theatre/English Touring Theatre and National tour); Sweeney Todd (Royal Festival Hall). Kay was resident at the West Yorkshire Playhouse for 17 years where she cast many shows including Hamlet, the McKellen Ensemble Season, the Patrick Stewart Priestley Season and many others, and also casts regularly for Salisbury Playhouse, Northampton Theatres (including Young America at the National Theatre), Liverpool Everyman and Playhouse, Hull Truck and the Manchester Library Theatre. She has just completed casting on Walk Like a Panther, a pilot TV for Finite Films. Kay is a member of the Casting Directors Guild of Great Britain (CDG).

Watford Palace Theatre...

is a local theatre with a national reputation.

The creative hub at the heart of Watford, the Palace engages people through commissioning, creating and presenting high-quality theatre, and developing audiences, artists and communities through exciting opportunities to participate. Contributing to the identity of Watford and Hertfordshire, the Palace enriches people's lives, increases pride in the town, and raises the profile of the area. The beautiful 600-seat Edwardian Palace Theatre is a Grade II listed building, busy with live performances and film screenings seven days a week, offering world-class art to the tens of thousands of people visiting the Theatre each year.

The quality of work on stage and beyond is central to the Theatre's ethos. Recently, the Palace has enjoyed critical acclaim for its productions of Julian Mitchell's Family Business (2011), Alan Ayckbourn's Time of My Life (2011), Gary Owen's Mrs Reynolds and the Ruffian (2010, TMA Best New Play nomination) and Neil Simon's Brighton Beach Memoirs (2010, TMA Best Supporting Performance in a Play nomination).

Work created at Watford Palace Theatre regularly tours nationally. Recent co-productions include Britain's Got Bhangra with Rifco Arts and Warwick Arts Centre, Tanika Gupta's Great Expectations with English Touring Theatre, The Human Comedy with the Opera Group and the Young Vic (nominated for the Evening Standard award for Best Musical), Marks and Gran's Von Ribbentrop's Watch with Oxford Playhouse and Stick Man with Scamp, which continues to tour nationally and internationally.

The Palace has commissioned and is producing new plays with a range of exciting writers including Charlotte Keatley's Our Father (2012) and Anthony Clark's Our Brother David (2012).

Projects such as Diwali (2011), Windrush (2010) and Hello, Mister Capello (2010) have brought together the creativity of Watford's diverse communities. These build on the regular programme of Palace and Hertfordshire County Youth Theatres, adult workshops, backstage tours, community choir and extensive work with schools.

A year in numbers...
- Reaching a total of 180,000 people
- Over 16,000 participatory sessions
- 177,000 unique website visits
- A pantomime attended by over 25,000 visitors
- More than 330 artists supported
- Visits generate over £1.2m of spending in the local economy
- Over 300 performances and 250 film screenings
- More than a dozen productions produced or co-produced
- Productions seen in more than 60 towns and cities across the UK

Watford Palace Theatre Creative Associates

Watford Palace Theatre extends the ambition and reach of its work through partnership projects and by offering developmental resources to the following Resident Companies and Creative Associates:

Resident Companies

Rifco Arts, a theatre company producing new writing celebrating British Asian culture

nabokov, a new writing theatre company from the Eastern region

Creative Associates

Alice Birch, a young playwright

Charlotte Keatley, an internationally acclaimed playwright best known for her hit play My Mother Said I Never Should

Gary Owen, an award-winning playwright whose work has been successfully produced nationally

Kate Flatt, an acclaimed international choreographer living in Watford and working around the world

The Opera Group, producing and touring quality music theatre and opera

Scamp Theatre, producers for the Eastern region specialising in work for young people

Stacey Gregg, an emerging playwright with a distinctive voice

Work created at and with Watford Palace Theatre regularly tours nationally. Productions you may have seen recently:

NowHere
choreographed by and co-produced with Divya Kasturi, which has toured nationally

Stickman
from the book by Julia Donaldson, co-produced with Scamp, which has toured internationally and played at London's Soho and Sound Theatres and the Edinburgh Festival

Bunny
by Jack Thorne, a Fringe First-winning production in association with nabokov and the Mercury Colchester, which has toured nationally and played at London's Soho Theatre and in New York

Family Business
a new play by Julian Mitchell, co-produced with Oxford Playhouse

Street Scene
Music by Kurt Weill, book by Elmer Rice, lyrics by Langston Hughes, co-produced with The Opera Group and the Young Vic, which won the Evening Standard award for Best Musical

Friend or Foe
by Michael Morpurgo, co-produced with Scamp Theatre

Britain's Got Bhangra
conceived and written by Pravesh Kumar, music by Sumeet Chopra, lyrics by Dougal Irvine, co-produced with Rifco Arts and Warwick Arts Centre

Young Pretender
by E. V. Crowe, co-produced with nabokov and Hull Truck Theatre in association with Mercury Colchester

Dusk Rings a Bell
by Stephen Belber, co-produced with Hightide Festival Theatre

Great Expectations
by Charles Dickens, adapted by Tanika Gupta, co-produced with English Touring Theatre

Be Part of Watford Palace Theatre

Circle Membership

Enjoy an even more special relationship with Watford Palace by becoming a Circle Member.

Palace Circle £20 (£30 for two people with the same address)
- 10% off top-price tickets
- 20% off 'Palace Tuesdays'
- Priority brochure mailing
- Regular Circle Newsletter
- No charge for postage on tickets bought by phone
- No exchange fee when changing tickets to another performance of the same show

Directors' Circle £175

All Palace Circle benefits plus
- Private backstage tours
- Acknowledgement in our show programmes
- Invitations to special events with artists working on productions

Participation

Unique opportunities for people young and old to engage with creative arts and get involved in the work of their local theatre.

Cultural Celebrations

A series of celebratory events marking key moments in the calendar of Watford's local communities including Black History Month, Chinese New Year, Vaisakhi, Eid and Diwali.

Rumour

Watford Palace Theatre's free membership scheme for 16–25s, offering discounted theatre and film tickets and access to exclusive events.

Other New Writing at Watford Palace Theatre

**Mrs Reynolds and the Ruffian
by Gary Owen**

**Great Expectations
by Charles Dickens
adapted by Tanika Gupta**

**Family Business
by Julian Mitchell**

**Our Brother David
by Anthony Clark**

Follow us:

Supported by
ARTS COUNCIL
ENGLAND

Our Father

Playwright's Comment

They say 'write about what you know'; but we all know more than we think we do. To write this play I set off on a journey into a forest of things I didn't understand, to explore, listen, encounter them and try to find a way through and out of the other side. Some scenes of this play came into my head eighteen years ago, but I couldn't understand what they added up to – a young woman talking to me from her cell in a medieval village . . . a woman speaking as her six-year-old self . . . a daughter and father by a huge dam surrounded by hills scorched with drought . . . Then three years ago I sensed what this play is, and Brigid Larmour said, write it.

Writing plays is not something I do on my own in a room, I walk and live it and put myself into the situation of the characters as much as I can, in order to understand how they feel both physically and emotionally. I believe I have to take the risk with myself first, otherwise how can I expect the actors to follow me there, or you the audience to be moved to laugh and cry.

I'm often scared and lost writing a play, because I follow images that come to me and pull on the rope of words and stories attached, and out they all come – things I don't even want to write about, but my hunch is, I have to try.

I think a good play is a healing experience if we get it right, because we can stare at our worst fears but also our deepest hopes, act them out, witness who we might be, who we want to be, who we dare to become.

For this play I went to places and people who have developed ways to heal and resolve the emotional, physical and psychological wounds that run through most families. I've tried to write a play about the way we all carry damage that has happened to people in our families – for generations – until the story is let out and the hurt is acknowledged and can be released. There seems to me a deep parallel between this and the way we treat the earth we live on.

The reason I wanted to write this play for Brigid Larmour is that she has such faith in playwrights as the reinventors of theatre. It is a very rare kind of theatre director who wants you to fulfil the potential of your own intuition, rather than write the kind of play she or he knows how to direct. Brigid and I are also rigorous at examining every line of the text, the exactness of structure and rhythm, as I craft the play. And everyone here at Watford Palace Theatre is fired with this same collaborative generosity. Suddenly as a playwright I am not alone any more, but in a buzzing creative environment.

Playwrights are often asked to explain 'what it's about' but Brigid asks 'what do you need?'. From early on I wanted to try out scenes or fragments with actors, so Brigid made that happen. I haven't worked from a conventional plot, I never write chronologically; I built up this play and its world by recognising the truth of the story as it appeared: trying out what seemed like the potent scenes with actors and taking my bearings from these. And rewriting and rewriting to make the play as vivid and as inhabitable as possible for the actors and audience. Literally every word has been tested and questioned aloud by Brigid and myself: we share a fanatic appreciation that the word in theatre is not only the source of meaning and poetry, but must trigger actions, gestures, sounds and unforgettable images.

This play includes the flooding of a landscape, a scene underwater, scenes 800 years ago – Brigid never says 'no', she says 'this is going to be a really exciting play'. I hope so. We have all been working together towards this moment of performance, because the full meaning of a play only emerges at the moment the play is received by the audience. Thank you for coming.

Thanks

To Brigid Larmour for her absolute faith in my ability especially when I doubted it.

To Annette Bond, Jamie de Courcey, Niamh Dowling, Andrea Hutcheson and my Mum, for supporting me through the most traumatic experiences of research for this play.

To Mark Crowfoot for introducing me to Atlow Mill Centre for Emotional Healing; and to all at Atlow Mill for their warmth and support, especial thanks to Jean Bond for her extraordinary guidance which helped me so much.

To the group with whom I did a Family Constellation Therapy workshop at the Chiron centre in London in November 2009. To Frank Marjisson and Sue Hampton for their wise counsel.

To Jenny Howe, Paul Mitchell, and Ian Reid, each of whom read some of my many drafts and gave me expert feedback, and supported and encouraged me in the writing process.

To all the actors who read and tried out scenes of this play along the way, in Manchester and at Watford. To NWPlaywrights for the writers' retreat in 2009. To the third-year students I taught at Manchester University, who volunteered to workshop some scenes with me in December 2011 and gave invaluable insights. To the actors and production team here at WPT who are making this play come alive for the first time.

And most of all, to my daughter Georgia, thank you for cooking your tea so often when I was still writing, and for your amazing spirit, wit and companionship – to you I dedicate this play.

Charlotte Keatley
Manchester, January 2012

Characters

Anna – *age nearly thirty in the present. Born 1982. Brought up in the Peak District and Manchester.*

Bill – *Anna's father. Age sixty-seven in the present. Born 1945 in Yorkshire, now a retired engineer living by two reservoirs in the Peak District, where he worked in the 1970s. Married to Sheila.*

Sheila – *Anna's mother. Age sixty-two in the present. Born 1950 in village of Whitwell, now drowned by a reservoir. Married to Bill. Schoolteacher in the new village of Landcross, soon to retire.*

Catherine – *age fifteen, a shepherdess living in Whitwell 800 years before, who becomes an Anchoress – a religious recluse.*

Jack – *age thirty-three in the present. Born 1979 in this area but brought up in various places across the north of Britain. Doubles with* **Priest** *in scenes with Catherine the Anchoress.*

Setting

2012, a fiercely hot and dry summer in the Peak District of England, in a remote valley. A sense of enormous landscape: hills, sky, reservoir and dam; silence and eternity. There is a drought: the hills are burnt brown, the reservoir is a third empty.

All the times and places of the scenes should co-exist in a non-naturalistic set. We see a section of the stone edge of the middle dam, which can be walked on; and at times characters enter the water.

For the scenes in Sheila and Bill's house: there are no walls, we see the landscape behind the house; we only need a kitchen sink, an upright fridge freezer about fifteen years old, and a table – all of which could be part of some non-naturalistic form in the landscape.

For the house we need a back kitchen door to outside, and a bedroom door, but not walls, except in the old bedroom where we need a sense of the thick, old stone walls. The stone-walled cell of the Anchoress can use the same wall, the rest of the walls can be delineated with light.

It is possible that everything stone or wall or dam is represented by the same sculptural abstract mass, so that when the house is destroyed at the end, we have the sense of all the walls in this play being breached.

Props in the script should be naturalistic.

Act One

Scene One: Reservoir

2012. A huge reservoir surrounded by hills in the Peak District, northern England. Dawn, midsummer day. **Anna** *in a summer dress stands on the raised parapet of the dam wall, water on the drop on the other side. Below, on the grass edging the dam wall, is a bundle of tent, sleeping bag, and backpack.*

Anna   Hills and reservoir and huge sky. Midsummer day. Everything perfect. Except me, I've ruined it . . .

Jack *enters, coming from the hillside, walks along the grass below* **Anna**. *She hasn't seen him yet.*

Anna   Anna you stupid idiot, you stupid fucker, you fucking useless fucker – you've lost him! Why why why why why?

Jack   Can I help?

Anna   – Oh!

Jack   Didn't mean to scare you. Are you okay?

Anna (*slight pause*)   Yes.

Jack   Who have you lost?

Anna (*hesitates*)   My boyfriend.

Jack   Couples are always splitting up here. They come out here thinking it's romantic, the edge of the great dam. But the silence is too big for most people. City people especially. It exposes you.

Slight pause.

Or the reservoir is cursed.

Anna   Did you see a van, in the lay-by over there?

Jack   No. And I was up on the hill before dawn.

Anna   He must've gone back to Manchester in the night.

Jack   That's not very nice, is it?

Anna   It was my fault . . .

Jack   Was it? (*Slight pause*.) He didn't need to leave you in the middle of nowhere. Do you want a lift to the station?

Anna   No. I'm staying here.

Jack (*slight pause*)   You're not supposed to camp here, you know.

Anna   Is that any of your business?

Jack   Yes. I'm a ranger for the area. (*Gestures*.) Green shirt.

Anna   Well my grandfather built this dam. He used to bring me up here to have picnics. I'm not doing any harm, am I? – I'm not polluting the water.

Jack   I have to check people don't chuck stuff in the reservoir.

Anna   Like what?

Jack   Themselves.

Anna   I'm not going to. (**Anna** *balancing*.)

Jack   – Please don't fall.

Anna   I'm a very strong swimmer.

Jack   The water is low because of the drought, I don't want you to get hurt.

Anna *sits down on the wall to talk to him.*

Anna   – Why were you up on the hill at dawn?

Jack (*slight pause*)   I was meditating. Summer solstice.

Anna   And you came down here for a spliff.

Jack   I came to measure the water level.

Anna   Did you hear the thunder? Thought it was going to rain.

Jack Hasn't rained for forty-two days.

Anna Please can you pass me that water.

Jack If you get down.

Anna *climbs down the wall,* **Jack** *fetches the water bottle.*

Jack It's empty.

Anna Great. Mike finished that too.

Jack (*slight pause*) Would you like some tea?

Anna I don't drink tea.

Jack *unpacks thermos, cups and old decorated tin, and pours tea, during:*

Jack It's nettle tea. I picked the leaves in the wood down there.

Anna What is this, hippy mountain rescue?

Jack I keep stuff in the landrover. I'm out on the moors all day.

Anna Lucky you. I like this old tin. (*Reads:*) 'J . . .'

Jack – Jack. (*Slight pause.*) Anna . . . I heard you.

Anna . . . Did you. (*Slight pause.*) And what do you keep in here?

Jack Flapjacks. Want one?

Anna I don't eat biscuits.

Jack Homemade.

He gives cup of tea to **Anna**.

Anna I'm going to see my parents and Mum will be cooking a huge lunch . . . She's expecting me and Mike. (*Big sigh.*)

Jack Maybe he'll come back today?

Anna   No. Last night we had a – massive row . . . it got dark
. . . I sat and looked at the stars, and I must have fallen
asleep.

Jack (*slight pause*) . . . I've been there. Looking at the stars
helps.

Anna   Yes. (*Pause.*) We'd been doing up a house together.
I'm thirty in a few weeks and my life has fallen apart. –
Sorry. Why do you work out here?

Jack   I like solitude.

Anna   I like it because it's so empty.

Jack   There are stories in the land, if you look carefully.

Anna   Like what?

Jack   The hillsides have shrunk in the heat – at dawn and
dusk the shadows mark the old settlements.

Anna   Medieval. It was warmer then, they grew different
crops.

Jack   You know about that?

Anna (*slight pause*)   Up on Edge Moor there are field
patterns three thousand years old.

Jack   Will you show me?

Anna   Maybe. They're special. They give out something . . .
When everything else has gone wrong, I come back here.

Jack   Does that happen often?

Anna (*slight pause*)   I don't need rescuing.

Jack   Okay. (*Slight pause.*) Just tell me when you want a lift
to the station. Sheffield, your parents? Or Manchester?

Anna   No. They live over there.

Jack   The house on the shore?

Anna   It has an amazing view over the water – you can see
all the sky and hills reflected. My Grandad built it.

Jack   He took a risk. What if the reservoir flooded?

Anna   He said it can't. He built the house, the dam, and the overflow system. (*Slight pause.*) But he didn't think about the reservoir drying up. It looks odd, stranded there above the mud.

Jack   I was up by the house last week, checking the water pipe that goes up to it. Your Dad came out to ask what I was doing. He was pretty surly. Your Mum was polite, in an English way.

Anna   Dad's a bit possessive about the place . . .

Jack   Why?

Anna   He came here in the seventies, raised the height of the dam and doubled the size of the reservoir.

Jack   All by himself.

Anna   You know what I mean.

Jack   And your Grandfather said, I now give you permission to marry my daughter . . .

Anna   Sort of.

Jack   So now what – you build an even bigger dam?

Anna   No point. No rain. We've fucked the climate – it's either drought or floods. Reservoirs can't cope with that. Across the world, dams are turning farmland into dust. Half the rivers in the world no longer reach the sea. (*Slight pause.*) If you care about the land –

Jack   – I do –

Anna   – You wouldn't work here.

Jack   Yes! You're an echo of me.

Anna   How?

Jack   I've come here because the reservoir's going to dry up completely, this summer. And . . .

Anna   And?

Jack   . . . I want to heal the land.

Anna (*pause*)   That's a big one. (*Slight pause.*) I've come here to sort myself out.

Jack   It's all connected.

Takes from his bag and unfolds a large sheet of paper.

Jack   We're looking for answers.

Anna   Are there any . . .?

Jack   I've started making a map.

Anna   Not much on it –

Jack   – Of ancient places we've forgotten . . .

Anna   What does that say?

Jack   – Well spring.

Anna   There are more standing stones than you've got . . . There's a handfast stone on Edge Moor – here . . . What's this mark, by the reservoir?

Jack   That's where I was born.

Anna   On the hillside?

Jack   There were caravans and huts here when they raised the dam wall. My Mum served hamburgers from a van. And my Dad was digging in the mud. Doing the hard graft. It wasn't just people like your Dad, with clipboards.

Anna   Yeah okay I didn't mean –

Jack   Some people get completely forgotten – it pisses me off!

Anna (*slight pause*)   Did he tell you much about it?

Jack   No. Never.

Anna   Why not?

Jack   He went. After I was born.

Anna   . . . And where is he now, your Dad?

Jack   I don't know.

Slight pause.

Anna   Is that why you said this place is cursed?

Jack   Something down there under the water has been damaged.

Anna   You mean the village. Whitwell.

Jack   What do you know about it?

Anna   My Mum was born there – went to school there, for a year. Before they moved everyone to Landcross.

Jack   Does she remember it?

Anna   She was very small . . . She remembers them flooding it – the trees and houses slowly disappearing. I used to imagine everyone swimming underwater at school, and books floating down the corridors. You know when you've heard a story so many times it becomes a memory.

Jack   Some of us remember things we didn't see.

Anna (*slight pause*)   There's a medieval church down there.

Jack   Is there?

Anna   My Grandad saved what he could. They dug up the graves and moved them to the new village.

Jack   Under the church there'll be something older. Christians built on Pagan sites of worship.

Anna   Such as?

Jack   A sacred spring.

Anna   That's hard to find – water buried under water.

Jack   When the reservoir dries up, we'll see the whole site.

Anna   But how will you know if there was a spring, if it's dried up?

Jack   There'll be a well stone with cup holes carved in it. Put there to honour a sacred source of water.

Anna   And if you find it, what will happen?

Jack   If we make contact with it – energy will be released . . . things happen in subtle ways . . . It's bigger than us, we don't understand. We want instant results . . . but that's not how things heal deeply.

Anna   This is what I was trying to say to Mike – but he got fed up with – (*Stops.*) I'd better go now, or I'll be late.

Jack   – Anna?

Anna   What –

Jack (*hesitates*)   . . . Mike was the wrong person for you.

Anna   No, I'm crap, and – I was crap with Mike, a bit loony to be honest, and –

Jack   – Why do you think everything's your fault?

Anna   (*pause*) Do I? Look, I'm in a weird state today.

Jack   No, you're – you're you.

Anna   Don't.

Jack (*slight pause*)   I'll give you a lift then. Let me carry your rucksack. You look wasted.

Anna   Can I have one of your flapjacks . . .

Jack   Take the whole tin.

Anna   How will I get it back to you?

Jack   We'll find each other.

Anna   You think . . .?

Jack   We have already. Did you love him?

Anna (*slight pause*)   I don't know.

Jack   That's why he's gone. Don't be sad.

Anna   Why?

Jack   It would be easy to fall in love with you.

Blackout.

Scene Two: Doubt

Midday of same day, 21 June 2012. The kitchen of **Sheila** *and* **Bill***'s house. Beyond is the view of hills and reservoirs. A back door leads straight into the kitchen.* **Sheila** *putting finishing touches to a bowl of salad.* **Bill** *examining the back of the fridge. A watering can near the back door. A row of tomato seedlings on a windowsill.*

Anna *has just entered, in the dress as in previous scene, carrying her backpack and sleeping bag, which she puts down by the door.*

Bill   Hello Anna, running away to the circus?

Anna   Hi Dad. Hi Mum.

Sheila   Where's Mike?

Anna   He's not coming.

Pause.

Sheila   He's left you, hasn't he.

Anna   Yes.

Sheila   Oh Anna. Oh love, come here.

Bill   You drive them away, don't you. What was it this time?

Sheila   Mike wasn't the one.

Anna   How do you know?

Sheila   I could feel in my bones.

Anna   Why didn't you tell me?

Sheila   I don't like to interfere, love.

Bill   He seemed a nice bloke. I thought you were going to have babies.

Anna   So did I.

Sheila   You're better off without children. Is he keeping the house?

Anna   Obviously. It's his.

Sheila   But you did all that work on it . . . Where are you going to live?

Anna   I don't know.

Bill   Well you can't make an encampment in the kitchen.

Anna   I'll move it.

Carries rucksack and bags across room.

Sheila   Let her have a wash first. You must be very upset.

Anna   Can I have some water?

Bill   You don't have to ask.

Anna *turns on the tap, fills a glass.*

Anna   Is our supply alright then?

Sheila   You know what Father said – the deepest spring in Derbyshire, it'll never run dry.

Bill   He must've known something we don't. People in Sheffield will be drinking their own piss soon.

Anna   I've never seen the reservoir so low.

Bill   It was bad that summer you botched your A levels.

Anna   Leave it, Dad. – Okay?

Bill   We're all hot. And hungry.

Sheila   In Landcross village they're rationing water. Lots of the children at school haven't had a bath in weeks.

Anna   Same in Manchester. I can't water the school allotments, everything's dying.

Bill *picks up his watering can from beside the back door.*

Sheila   Can't you fill that from the outside tap?

Bill   The hose is on the outside tap, to water the beans. I need this for the tomatoes.

Sheila   They can wait till after lunch.

Bill   No they can't, they've waited long enough already.

Sheila   Don't blame me.

Bill   – You asked me to look at the fridge! You thought it was de-frosting.

Sheila   I didn't say take the back off.

Bill   There was a puddle underneath.

Sheila (*to* **Anna**)   Your Dad . . . Now that he's retired he never stops taking things apart.

Bill   Oh, rub salt in it! Just as well I've got time on my hands, there's always something leaking in this house. Might as well live at the bottom of the sea.

Anna   I'll help you water the tomatoes, Dad. I love the smell of the leaves.

Bill (*pleased*)   If you want, Annie.

Sheila   I'm putting this salad on the table and then it's lunch in five minutes.

Bill   So hot this year, I've got a second crop going in here see.

Sheila   Anna don't put your bags here, I can't get in the dining room.

Anna *drags rucksack and bags across the room again.*

Anna   Are we eating in there?

Sheila   I thought as Mike was coming –

Slight pause.

Bill (*to* **Anna**) You could've phoned this morning. Your mother's done a special lunch.

Anna   Sorry.

Sheila   I don't know how you managed all that baggage by yourself.

Bill   That clod who thinks he's a ranger gave her a lift. – Saw his landrover from the bathroom window.

Sheila   That's nice of him.

Bill   Don't have anything to do with him, Anna.

Anna   Why?

Sheila   Your Dad's nose is out of joint.

Sheila *exits into the dining room, carrying salad.* **Bill** *waters seedlings.*

Bill   He knows nothing about land drainage. He's a lost soul looking to find his identity. I'll be surprised if he finds it on a drought-stricken hillside.

Bill *hums 'Jerusalem' for a moment, watering the seedlings.*

Anna   Dad – (*Stops.*)

Bill   What, Annie?

Anna   Don't you ever have doubts? About your life?

Bill   Doubt is for no-hopers. Your Mum and I have always been very happy.

Anna   Have you?

Bill   You've never heard us have a row, have you?

Lights change to near dark, pouring rain outside. **Anna** *and* **Bill** *are no longer on stage.* **Sheila** *enters from the house, in her winter dressing gown, carrying a torch. It is now 2 a.m., an April night in*

2002. **Bill** *is aged 57,* **Sheila** *is aged 52,* **Anna** *is aged 20. Noises outside the back door.*

Sheila   . . . Bill? Is that you? – Bill? . . . Who's out there?

Bill *opens the kitchen back door and enters shaking a large wet umbrella.*

Bill   Of course it's me. Who else would it be at two in the morning?

Sheila   Well I don't know – I jumped awake.

Bill   Decided to come home early. What's happened to the lights?

Sheila   A power cut. Must be the storm.

Bill   Torrential out there. April showers – ha ha . . . Desperate driving home, could hardly see through the windscreen, roads like rivers.

Sheila   You're dripping everywhere –

Bill   Can a man not come in his own house!

Sheila   Please don't shout.

Sheila *grabs the umbrella and puts it outside the back door.*

Bill   I'm not shouting! Can't see a thing – Give me the torch –

Bill *takes the torch and opens fridge door.* **Sheila** *shuts back door.*

Bill   Where's that bowl of soup –

Sheila   I threw it out.

Bill   You didn't.

Sheila   It wasn't enough for a meal.

Bill   It's just what I want right now.

Sheila   The power is off, anyway.

Bill (*hunting in fridge*)   Where's that cold lamb?

Sheila   I don't know dear. I'd have saved you some shepherd's pie if I'd known you were coming back tonight.

Bill   Couldn't stay at the conference a moment longer. That new bastard, Drew – what kind of a name is that? – has stolen my idea and put it in his report to the company!

Sheila   Perhaps he had the idea at the same time.

Bill   Drew, have an original idea?! What's in these boxes . . . – Hold the torch so I can see, Sheila – Ah, here it is (*Lifts lid off a plastic pot.*) – No, that's cheese . . . what's happened to my labelling system! This is clearly marked cold lamb, and there's a piece of Wensleydale inside!

Sheila   Don't be so gnarly.

Bill   You'd be gnarly if you worked with rogues who thieved your ideas all the time.

Sheila   Gerry is always nice to you.

Bill   Gerry is an utter twit! – Lets them walk all over him and goes on smiling!

Sheila   Father would say, 'Turn the other cheek.'

Bill   Sheila, both my cheeks are black and blue.

Sheila   Can you close the fridge door now or everything will de-frost.

Bill   – It needs de-frosting. Look at it – glaciers seizing up the drawers.

Sheila   Not tonight, please Bill –

Bill   Well, what else can I do, to unwind after a hard day's work?!

Deafening silence.

Sheila   I need to sleep on my own at the moment. I can't sleep otherwise . . . What do you want me to say, Bill.

Bill There's nothing to say. I'm clearly not good enough for you.

Sheila (*slight pause*) Why are you home tonight?

Bill – What?

Sheila Was . . .

Bill I was at a conference in Harrogate, as you well know.

Sheila – Was she there?

Bill She –? – Give me that torch – That's bloody manipulative, that is! – Wait, Anna's sneaking about – Oy! What are you doing downstairs?

Anna *enters the scene.*

Anna Hello Dad.

Bill What are you wearing?

Anna It's what I sleep in.

Bill Where's the bottom half?

Anna There isn't a bottom half. It's a big tee shirt.

Bill This is not a student house.

Anna It's too hot in this house.

Bill Your mother needs it like that, doesn't she.

Sheila Can't you sleep?

Anna I was up. Working on my dissertation.

Bill (*holds out pot*) Did you put the cheese in here?

Anna No . . . I put apple crumble leftovers in that pot yesterday –

Bill You've been rummaging around, haven't you!

Anna Dad –

Bill Well don't. This is my house, this is not your house!

Sheila She's probably worried about her finals.

Bill (*to* **Anna**)   You've caused me enough myther,
losing the front-door key. All this to-ing and fro-ing from
university –

Anna   – I come here so Mum isn't alone when you're away.

Bill   She can phone me! What are mobiles for?

Anna   If Mum has one of her panic attacks, I want to be
here.

Bill   – And bringing your boyfriends round –

Anna   Joe gave me a lift here Dad, and Ben is a friend –

Bill   – Don't know who I might find wandering round my
home, or who's got a key to this place –

Sheila   Don't say that! I won't sleep. Did you get a
new lock?

Bill   Yes, and brand-new keys. So you know that only you
and I can get in this house. Alright? Alright now?

Sheila   Stop it Bill.

Bill   . . . It's not normal, Sheila!

Anna   It's alright Mum . . .

Sheila   Uh – uh . . . (*Dizzy.*)

Anna   It's because you didn't eat supper.

Sheila   I wasn't hungry. I'm going to lie down.

Sheila *exits.*

Anna   Call if you need me Mum!

Pause.

Bill   All these boyfriends of yours, worry her sick.

Anna   – She didn't say that.

Bill   No, she wouldn't. Wants you to do what you want . . .

Anna   I'll come on my own then, from now on.

Bill   How will you do that?

Anna   Get the train and walk from the station. – Are you going to give me a key?

Bill *gets out a key for* **Anna***.*

Bill   You'd better not lose this one. I got them cut specially – look. – I missed an hour of the conference, going out to find a key cutter in Harrogate.

Anna   You should've got your P.A. to do it.

Bill (*pause*)   Yes – well – she had to go early.

Anna   Thanks, Dad. I'll go and see if Mum's okay.

As **Anna** *exits:*

Bill   That'll be three pounds twenty-five pence.

Lights change, and come up bright for the hot day in the present as before.

Bill *no longer wears the coat but is dressed as before and is watering the seedlings while humming 'Jerusalem'.*

Bill (*calls*)   Anna, have you got the plant food? It's the brown bottle – an old lemonade bottle – labelled 'tomato feed', obviously –

Sheila *re-enters from dining room, dressed as in first part of scene.*

Sheila   It's boiling in there, I thought I asked you to open the windows?

Bill   There was a fly.

Sheila *picks up window key and exits to dining room again as* **Anna** *re-enters from the back door, dressed as in first part of scene, carrying a bottle.*

Bill   Ah that's it.

Anna   You shouldn't use a chemical feed, Dad. I can make you one, rot down nettles, I was showing the kids.

Bill   How's it going, your Green Fingers whatsit project?

Anna   The City Council has cut our budget for the autumn.

Bill   By how much?

Anna   Completely. (*Pause.*) Five years' work down the drain.

Bill   But you won that prize last year. – The Council put a photo of you on their brochure!

Anna   Teaching kids how to grow vegetables isn't essential, is it . . . Another of my deluded ideas.

Bill (*pause*)   So you're looking for a job?

Anna (*pause*)   I don't how to go on living.

Bill   Now now. If you start doubting yourself, everything falls apart.

Slight pause.

Anna   The world is heading for meltdown. What's the point of a job? I have nightmares where everything has turned to desert.

Bill   You need a thinner duvet. Five tog in heat like this.

Anna   You don't take me seriously, do you?

Bill   I've put a brick in the toilet cistern, what else do you want me to do – rend my clothes and rub ash on my head?

Anna   Don't you have doubts about – the whole way we live?

Bill   That degree in Environmental Science did you no good.

Anna   We're sleepwalking.

Bill   I've worked all over the world Anna, I've helped people to put things in place to cope with climate change –

Anna   Oh right – the dams you've built – they've caused more damage –

Bill   – That's going too far! (*Pause.*) I have my own beliefs, Anna. And I've done something in the world. And I made a home for you and your mother.

Anna And you think I'm a failure. No job, no kids, no – man in my life.

Bill I can't help you if you've got that attitude.

Sheila *re-enters from the dining room.*

Sheila (*to* Bill) Did you put a jug in the fridge to chill?

Bill You didn't ask me to.

Anna's *mobile phone beeps, she gets it out of her pocket and reads text.*

Bill *blasts the tap on, to run it cold.*

Bill It's cold enough. Coming from the bowels of the earth.

Sheila I wish you wouldn't use that expression. And will you push the fridge back where it was.

Anna *is texting a reply.*

Sheila Don't reply if he's going to upset you.

Anna It's not Mike. I texted Caz to see if I can stay at her house for a while.

Bill Another sofa bed. Another house where no one has a surname.

Sheila Which one is Caz? The one with the dog?

Anna No, she works with kids in care. (*Mobile beeps.*) Shit. . . She's got a friend staying, from Australia . . .

Sheila Well – stay here a few days, while you sort yourself out.

Bill It'll take more than a few days.

Anna Dad!

Bill I'm joking! Can't we have a joke round here?

Sheila Stay as long as you need love.

Anna Thanks Mum.

Bill *heaving the fridge back to the wall, sees something in the dust.*

Bill   Well look what I've found. The front-door key. From years ago.

Anna   That new one you got me?

Bill   You can use it while you're here.

A beat. **Anna** *accepts the key.*

Anna   Thanks.

Bill   You still owe me three pounds twenty-five.

Sheila   Well, there's a cold chicken in the next room, I don't know why we're all stood here.

Anna   If you don't mind, I'll go and have a shower . . . I'm not really hungry.

Bill   Anna – your mother's put a lot of trouble into the lunch.

Blackout.

Scene Three: Faith

The year 1212. Early January. A solemn bell sounds. The interior of the village church in Whitwell; it is simply a high dark space, as it is still night. As the **Priest** *enters carrying a candle, we see a shape on the floor, a mound of heavy clothing, muddy and worn but thick layers of it.*

Priest (*crosses himself*)   Hast thou life?

The mound moves. **Catherine**, *who was prostrate in prayer, raises her head: we see her face.*

Cath   Forgive me Father. Oft' I spend the nights here . . . in prayer.

Priest   Art thou Catherine, who minds the sheep?

Cath   Aye! – I've been here all night, waiting on you.

Priest   I reached this village late last night and went to the Priest's house. It was a long ride from York Minster.

Cath – I thought you'd be old, being a Bishop.

Priest I am not the Bishop.

Cath Oh.

Priest He has appointed me to be Curate here. I am to be thy confessor and to instruct thee in the rules for becoming an Anchoress.

Cath – And did the Bishop say –?

Priest I have the Bishop's blessing to enclose thee in a cell, as thou hast asked – to be an Anchoress of this church.

Cath – Thanks be to God the Father! Oh such joy – I am full of it.

Priest And meekness, Catherine!

Cath . . . Aye. But gladness, 'tis rarer than meekness, think you not. – See the red crack of dawn, at the east window!

Priest Be frugal with thy words. Once she begins, a woman's tongue cackles like a hen. (*Pause.*) Art thou certain of this path? Thou must live in solitude for the rest of thy life.

Cath (*pause*) I crave it.

Priest As I am new to this village I know little of thy humours. To be always alone, can bring out the bile and the melancholic in the blood.

Cath Nay – I'm most oft' alone and glad o' it. Up ont' moors all day, minding us flock. Now't but sky, wind and moors.

Priest Then why dost thou seek to be walled in a cell?

Cath To give my life to God.

Priest For what?

Cath (*slight pause*) In penance for my sins.

Priest For what sins?

Cath (*pause*)   I am not worthy of this life.

Priest   None of us are worthy. That is why we begin each day with repentance to Almighty God.

Cath   And 'tis hard to pray with the sheep runnin' round me and the wind blowin' my words.

Priest   The Lord hears thee on the hill. Rebecca went into the wilderness to pray.

Cath   Aye, but she had no sheep to mind. Oft' when I sing praises to Our Father, the sheep are wont to start singing with me. (*Pause.*) Our Lady were alone, in prayer, when the angel came to her. A woman must give hersen' entirely to Our Father.

Priest   The walls of thy cell can never be opened until thy death, Catherine . . .

Cath   Aye. When may I be put in there?

Priest   The men of the village are bringing stones from the hill, and the stonemason awaits my orders.

Cath   – They'll be right powfagged after. How will my cell be – like a cow byre?

Priest   It will be a stone room against the church wall, near the altar. There will be a window into the church so I can give thee Communion. And another window looking on to the world thou hast left.

Cath   – I've no need of that.

Priest   – For food, water and clothing. Will thy father provide?

Cath   My sisters will bring me all I need.

Priest   The window to the outside will have a black shutter with a white cross. If it be not thy sisters or myself who comes to thy window, thou must close the shutter.

Cath   I only want to peep out at the sky, now and then.

Priest   No, Catherine! For if thou showest any part of thyself to a man, thou wilt open a pit wherein he may fall. For a man is like a bear, he cannot help but fall into the pit if a woman opens it before him. (*Slight pause.*) And if he falls, then it is the woman who is damned.

Cath   I have no wish to see any man. – Father see how the sun bobs up at altar window – a round mouth in heaven, calling the new day!

Priest (*slight pause*)   Thou art young. (*Pause.*) Hath thy father given permission for thee to be enclosed?

Cath (*pause*)   He has no need of me. My sisters can mind the sheep.

Priest   I am told thy mother lies in her grave, bless her soul.

Cath   In this village you'll find many folk lie cold in't ground. Three winters back e'en the well froze!

Priest   We shall pray for God's mercy this winter.

Cath   Amen to that.

Priest   Art thou sound in body?

Cath   I'm wick and fettle – I can run up hills faster than any man.

Priest   No man may enter thy cell, even if thou art sick.

Cath   Aye. Build the walls good and strong.

Priest (*pause*)   I will tell the stonemason to begin. Thou must go and make good all thy farewells.

Cath   Gladly.

Priest   Let us pray.

Father Almighty, we offer thee the life of Catherine, to be enclosed as an Anchoress, and set apart from mankind for her sins.

Cath (*a deep sigh*)

Priest   – Do you have any desires to confess?

Cath   Aye – (*Pause.*) I've a girt hunger to behold the sea.

Priest   The sea is a long way off. Two days' ride.

Cath   Is it true, it has no edges, and goes till eternity?

Priest   The sea is boundless, but God's eternity is greater.

They exit. Sheep call on the hill. The dawn light continues to grow rosy and bright and then into a hot day, around the house, as we go into it.

Scene Four: Breakfast

The present, the house. Friday 26 June – five days after Scene Two, Doubt.

Bill *holds a tray of breakfast outside the door to the old bedroom.*

Anna *is in bed, asleep.*

Bill (*calls*)   Anna. (*No reply.*) Anna. ANNA.

Anna   . . . What?

Bill   – 'Hello Dad'?

Anna   . . . uh, what time is it?

Bill   Nearly three in the afternoon. As usual, this week.

Anna   It's so quiet here . . . Feel like I'm underwater.

Bill   Your room has thicker walls than the rest of the house, it's the old stone blocks. (*Slight pause.*) Will you open the door.

Anna   I just want to sleep.

Bill *pushes open the door and stands in the doorway.*

Bill   – You're wasting the whole week, Anna.

Anna   Where's Mum?

Bill Out at work. She'll be back from Landcross Primary at four-thirty. It's Friday.

Anna I feel wiped out.

Bill You need some food. I've brought you breakfast.

Anna Uh . . . Leave it outside.

Bill Will you get up please, because I'm stood here like patience on a monument.

Anna Why have you done all this?!

Bill You don't turn up for meals, then you're off out for hours, without a word to us.

Anna I'm okay Dad. Thanks . . . but –

Bill – Free-range eggs. Home-grown tomatoes. The bread is my own too – I make all our loaves now. Bread turns out to be fairly similar to making a good concrete – it's mostly about texture and timing.

Anna – Thanks I really don't want any.

Bill You'll waste away!

Anna I won't! . . . I've got something with me.

Bill Oh yes. What exactly?

Anna A tin of flapjacks.

Anna *goes back to bed.*

Bill I've had enough of this, frankly. You get up and wash your face, I'll put this in the microwave and heat it up again. The bathroom's along the – well you know where the bathroom is.

Anna Please leave me alone.

Bill And your mother's dressing gown is in the cupboard.

Anna . . . Where are my clothes?

Bill   I put them all in the wash.

Anna   – You came in my room, while I was asleep . . .?! Will you go away, so I can go to the bathroom.

Bill   Yes, as soon as you take this tray from me.

Anna   I don't want any breakfast. I want to go to the bathroom.

Bill   I'm not stopping you Anna.

Anna   What do you want me to do, jump out of the window?

Bill   Behave like a normal person and take this tray.

Anna   What is a normal person? Not us.

Bill   I see. I suppose the people you know don't eat breakfast.

Anna   We're not all weirdos. Dad, let me out.

Bill   Anna I was simply bringing you –

Anna   – I don't want it. (**Anna** *gets up, grabs the tray and puts it on the bed.*)

Bill   – Bringing your breakfast. Don't you –

Anna   Get out of my room!

Bill   You're getting ridiculous, hysterical!

Anna   Leave me alone! Go on! Go away!

Bill *starts growling.*

Anna   – Dad . . .?

Bill *is turning into a wolf.*

Anna (*scared and excited*)   Dad?

Bill *growls louder.*

Anna   It's the wolf!

Bill, *roaring, chases and catches* **Anna**, *who screams.*

Anna   No, Dad!

Bill   What shall I eat for my dinner?

Anna (*breathless*)   A little girl.

Bill   A little girl . . . How old are you?

Anna   Four and a half.

Bill   Four and a half! Wolves especially like little girls who are four and a half.

Anna   Are you going to eat me then?

Bill   Am I going to eat you?

Anna   Yes?

Bill   Am I?

Anna   Yes!

Bill   I'm going to roast you till you're tender.

He spins her around.

Anna (*giddy*)   Dad –

Bill   Are you cooked yet? Let's feel – nice and tender.

Anna   Oh – ooh – that tickles.

Bill   Just nice.

Anna   Ooh ooh.

Bill   A nice juicy little girl.

Anna   Stop.

Bill   For my tea.

Anna   Stop stop.

Bill   Yum yum.

Anna   Stop!

Bill   There.

Anna   Mam says, Mam says don't forget the gravy.

Bill   Did she? Did she say that? Well the big wolf likes gravy over everything.

Anna   Over the table?

Bill   Shh come on now, it's lunchtime, calm down. Do you need a cushion? Eat your dinner.

Anna   Mummy gives me a little fork.

Bill   Daddy will be mother because Mam's having a rest.

Anna   What do you mean, be mother?

Bill   That means I'll pour the tea.

Anna   We haven't got tea.

Bill   Look at that nice lamb that Mam cooked.

Anna   What are you for, Dad?

Bill   What do you mean? I bath you.

Anna   Only sometimes, when you're here.

Slight pause.

And you smack me.

Bill   Only sometimes. And tell you stories.

Anna   Tell me a story.

Bill   Eat up your lamb.

Anna   Mam said if I eat half . . .

Bill   If you eat half, then what?

Anna   What?

Bill   What what. Last year it was why why. Don't say what, it's rude.

Anna *picks at food.*

Anna   I'm only eating half.

Bill If you only eat half, then only half of you will grow.

Anna Which half?

Bill What?

Anna You said what.

Bill Eat.

Anna I can't eat all this.

Bill I'll cut it up for you.

Anna Dad, where are you going?

Bill Get back to your chair.

Anna Are you going to Leeds, for a meeting?

Bill No, I'm going in the kitchen to get a knife. Eat!

Anna Dad – why is Mam in bed?

Bill Because you wear her out. Come on.

Anna . . . It's got fat on it.

Bill What? I can't hear you sometimes.

Anna It's got fat on it.

Bill It hasn't.

Anna Look.

Bill That's because you let it go cold.

Anna I don't like lamb.

Bill Come on, Mam cooked that especially for you, you don't want her to be disappointed, do you?

Anna Mam lets me have cheese.

Bill I'm Mam right now.

Anna What do you mean? I'll go and ask her.

Bill – You're not to wake her, she needs her rest.

Anna   Mam.

Bill   It's cold because you're messing around. Put a bit in Anna.

Anna   I can't chew it.

Bill   Anna, don't you – Anna! Put that back in! Now, swallow it. Good girl. Another piece. Now, here's my watch, I'm putting it on the table, see – when the big hand is at the top, I want that plate empty.

Anna   . . . Or?

Bill   Or?

Anna   Or what?

Bill   THERE ISN'T AN OR WHAT! Jesus Anna, you drive me –

Anna   With Mam there's an or –

Bill   – To the LIMIT!

Beat. They return to their present ages. **Anna** *stands in her doorway.*

Bill   Are you always like this in the mornings? I'm not surprised Mike left you.

Anna   He didn't leave me, I left him.

Bill   Well you'll not find a replacement at this rate.

Anna   I don't want to.

She closes the door again.

They speak through the door.

Bill   You wanted to go to the bathroom didn't you?

Anna   I can't.

Pause.

Bill   Why?

Anna   If I open the door I'm going to smash that tray and start screaming.

Bill Go on then.

Anna (*quietly* – **Bill** *doesn't hear*) Daddy please hold me I'm so scared.

Bill Well that were very tidy.

Anna *opens the door.*

Bill Ah there you are.

Anna . . . Uh, dizzy.

Bill You're probably hyperventilating.

Anna I don't feel . . .

Bill Here you go.

Bill *offers the tray to* **Anna**.

Anna (*stares*) Dad . . . it's snowing.

Bill Snowing?

Anna In my head.

Lights change to the bright reflecting white of snow on the far hills and all around.

Scene Five: Wall

The Cell, 1212, January, a few days after Scene Three, Faith. Snow on the hills around. **Catherine** *is dressed in a simple robe which drowns her shape.*

She is barefoot. Fierce pride and joy with her new boundaries.

Cath Wall! WALL! – There are no doors and no windows, for I keep the shutter closed. Save a slit for air. (*Pause.*) My country . . . They can give me neither food nor water, unless I take it upon mysen' to open the shutter. Then they may pass vittles in. And I pass my shit out! No words. They cannot whelp a word from me. I roar – loud as an ox. But only in my head! – Ssh! (*Stops.*) Who's that? (*Pause.*) They come to this window and mummer away, half the village.

Steps of **Priest** *approaching, with a bundle.*

Cath   Aye, 'tis the Priest. I know his tread.

Cath *listens as* **Priest** *comes up to the window and stops.*

Cath   I can say nowt if I choose.

Priest   Sister Catherine.

Cath (*silence*)

Priest   Sister Catherine?

Cath (*pause*)   Who's there?

Priest   Father Langley.

Cath (*slight pause*)   Hold while I put the sneck up, 'tis frozen. I keep the shutter across at all times. Canst not be sure who might be prying. The Miller's daughter, she's a nazard.

Priest   Thy father asks me to come to thee.

Cath   Doth he? (*No reply.*) 'Tis night, or near enough.

Priest   He sent thee a blanket.

Cath   He sent it?

Priest   It snows.

Cath   Aye it snowed all the night and day.

Priest   Who told thee?

Cath   No one. Canst hear it. There's grand silence falls ont' village when it snows. Like the Brig o' Dead. Not a peep, save the Miller's dog at the far end. Ist' pond frozen? Do the sheep have hay?

Priest   Think not of earthly matters.

Cath   I do not. Yet even though I close my eyes, I see this and that.

Priest   What dost thou see?

Cath (*slight pause*)   A rock.

Priest   The rock of the tomb?

Cath   Nay . . . the girt rock by the well, where the sheep will be chafing – 'tis a place to shelter from the blowing snows.

Priest   Think only of Our Saviour Catherine.

Cath   I do. He was a shepherd. Is't a sin to think of the sheep when he said, thou art all my flock.

Priest   Wilt thou take this blanket, my feet freeze.

Cath   I've no need of it.

Priest   Do not seek suffering, Catherine. It will come to thee in God's time.

Cath   If I were up on t'hills in t'snow I'd have no need, I'd dig a pit wit' sheep and we'd all snug down. One time we were buried two days, they come and dug us out, when I jumped up my father thought it were a devil! – Forgive me Lord . . . – Put t'blanket on the sill, I will fetch it from there if I choose when thou'rt gone.

Priest (*hesitates*)   Dost have enough firewood? Catherine? (*Pause.*) If it snows again, I will bring more.

Priest *waits for a reply, but there is none; he goes.* **Cath** *listens to footsteps until he's a little way off.*

Cath   I have 'em here. In my head. All o'them. Every peak an' ridge, every stone an' hill edge. Where I've run an' run an' run. (*Pause.*) I can be still now. Still . . . Ssh . . . List – (*Silence.*) How the snow falls from heaven.

Light fades on **Catherine**'s *face, to darkness.*

Scene Six: Whitey Pebbles

The day after Breakfast scene 27 June 2012. Early afternoon, hot fierce light on the water and hills. Sheep call on the far hillside. **Jack** *is at the edge of the reservoir, on the dry mud, choosing stones to throw out across the water, when* **Anna** *walks over to him.*

Anna   What are you up to?

Jack   Anna! Are you okay?

Anna   Yes.

Jack   – I was worried about you.

Anna   Were you?

Jack   You look different.

Anna   Sorry. I didn't feel like coming out yesterday.

Jack   I waited ages in our usual place.

Anna   I wanted to stay in bed. I felt like I could stay there for ever.

Jack   I'm glad you didn't.

Anna (*slight pause*)   I thought you like being alone?

Jack (*slight pause*)   So did I . . . (*Pause.*) till now.

Beat.

Jack   I climbed up to Edge Moor this morning and there was a mist in all the valleys, as if the sea had come in the night.

Anna   And now it's so hot the hills are a haze.

Slight pause.

Do you think it's too late – what we've done to the earth?

Jack   It's never too late.

Anna   . . . I missed you.

Slight pause.

I feel so much better out here.

They kiss.

Jack   Have you told your Mum and Dad yet?

Anna   No.

Jack Don't they wonder where you go in the days?

Anna They're letting me stay at the house because I split up with Mike, and I've got nowhere to live. If I tell them I'm having fantastic sex on the hill every afternoon with a bloke I just met they'll freak out.

Jack They sound freaked out anyway.

Anna I'd have to move out. Live in my tent.

Jack I'd bring you food and water.

Anna You said I can't camp here.

Beat.

This is probably all a rebound . . .

Jack Do you think so?

Anna *says nothing.*

Jack You don't have to see me any more Anna –

Anna You want to stop?

Jack (*pause*) I think of you from the moment I wake. In my sleep I thought I was holding you.

Anna You are . . . Even when we're not together, I can feel you.

Jack . . . Something amazing is happening.

Anna What?

Jack Out there, in the middle of the water –

Anna I can't see anything.

Jack Watch this –

Anna – Don't break the surface –

Jack *throws a stone. It hits something, then a splash.*

Jack Did you see that?

Anna   Yes.

Jack   It hit something hard.

Anna   When I was fifteen, the church tower appeared.

Jack (*throws another stone*)   Got it! Stone on stone.

Anna   My bones are all whitey pebbles now.

Jack   What?

Anna   I don't know. Just came out.

Jack *is about to throw another stone.*

Anna   – Don't throw any more stones Jack.

Jack   Okay. Why?

Anna (*pause*)   Sometimes I hear this woman . . .

Jack   There are lots of voices around us. Most people don't hear them.

Anna   So you don't think I'm mad . . .?

Jack   No. Stones have memories.

Anna   How can they?

Jack   In an old house, have you ever felt – sad, or angry?
– Voices stay in walls.

Anna   It's just things you remember.

Jack   What if they're not your memories.

Anna   Now you're scaring me.

Jack   Don't be scared. Walls get broken up. Stones are moved. Voices get lost.

Anna *picks up a piece of stone.*

Anna   I wonder if this was part of a house in Whitwell . . .

Jack   It's a bit small.

Anna   – They bulldozed some of the village before they flooded it.

Jack Even the old church?

Anna Some of it.

Jack Christians are weird.

Anna My Grandad rescued as many stones as he could, and built an extension on our cottage. That's why the walls in my room are so thick . . . Feels very safe, nothing can get me there.

Jack I'll never hurt you Anna.

Anna Hold me.

Jack *does.*

Anna – Uh-uh-uh.

Jack What's up? Anna –

Anna (*sounds between choking and retching come out of her*)

Jack What is it? Can you breathe?

Anna Euch, euch.

Expels all the air in her lungs.

Jack Can you breathe?

Anna *nods, holds on to* **Jack**.

Jack I'm here, I'm here with you. Can you speak?

Anna (*breathing returns to normal*) . . . Yeah. Don't know – what that was.

Jack Fucking hell.

Anna – What?

Jack It came flooding in to me.

Anna What . . .

Jack The pain! White hot. Anna how do you put up with it?

Anna I don't feel any pain.

Jack   You don't . . .?

Anna   – And no one else has felt pain inside me.

Jack   Then they didn't love you enough.

Pause.

Jack   I want to help you – get it out of you.

Anna   You came here to heal the land.

Jack   I can't heal it without you.

Blackout.

Scene Seven: Sleepwalking

*The bedroom, 27 June 2012, middle of the night after previous
Scene Six, Whitey Pebbles.* **Anna** *in bed asleep in the near dark, but
some moonlight from the window.*

Sheila *walks in, moves about;* **Anna** *stirs in her sleep and drops
something she has been holding: the stone from the previous scene.
The sound wakes her and she sees* **Sheila** *standing there.*

Anna   – Mum?

Sheila   I'm looking for the box.

Anna   What box?

Sheila   My jewellery box.

Anna   Mum? Are you awake?

Sheila   Yes. Of course.

Anna   You scared me.

Sheila   I didn't mean to wake you.

Anna   Mum? Are you okay?

Sheila   Yes. Are you?

Anna   It's the middle of the night.

Sheila   Yes. Go back to sleep.

Sheila *moves around the room.*

Anna . . .What are you looking for?

Sheila I was lying in bed and I suddenly remembered my jewellery box, I thought, I've got something in there for Anna . . .

Anna What jewellery box?

Sheila What?

Anna What jewellery box?

Sheila I think you're dreaming.

Anna Me?

Sheila You're talking nonsense. I've mended your dress, where you tore the lace off the hem.

Anna Mum? What are you doing?

Sheila I often do little chores at night, if I can't sleep . . . You go back to your bed, and go to sleep.

Anna I am in bed.

Sheila You're a bad girl.

Anna (*pause*) Why . . .?

Sheila You know why.

Sheila *walks out of* **Anna**'s *room.*

Anna Mum?

Anna *closes her eyes and tries to sleep again. She remains in her bed in the darkness as we go into the next scene.*

Scene Eight: Serpents

The Anchoress's Cell. January 1212. Almost dark, a few tapers burn in the church; a bell tolls. **Priest** *comes to the window on the church side of the cell.*

Priest Catherine –

Cath   – Oh! – Thought you were a boggart . . .

Priest   I hear thee mewling. It disturbs my prayers.

Cath   Forgive me!

Priest   Hast thou anything to confess?

Cath *throws herself on her knees.*

Cath   Nay. I would vomit out venom, that lies across my heart.

Priest   What venom?

Cath   Of serpents that crawl through me.

Priest   These are sent to try thee. As Christ in the wilderness was taunted. It will pass.

Cath   I am like a sheep with worms. These serpents writhe and turn about in my head, all day long.

Priest   Then say the Our Father.

Cath   I do!

Priest   – Silently, and without moving.

Catherine *prays silently, tries to keep her body from shaking.*

Cath   – Leave me not! . . . Father.

Priest   The villagers are arriving in the church, for Vespers. (*Hesitates.*) I can bring thee the Holy Book, thou mayst read the scriptures for solace.

Cath   I am unlettered.

Priest   Canst thou make good needlework?

Cath   I'd make a juggins of it.

Priest   There are many empty hours in the life of an Anchoress –

Cath   – I hear best in the silence.

Priest (*pause*)   But if a woman does not have an occupation, the poisonous Serpent of Envy may enter her . . . and sow the seeds of Suspicion and Wrath.

Cath   – I'm afeared o' such a girt stinking mass of wickedness inside me!

Priest   Recite the seven penitential psalms . . . and one hundred Aves. Over and over. Fill the silence with your faith in Almighty God.

Blackout.

Scene Nine: Skipping

Garden of **Bill** *and* **Sheila***'s house, hot Saturday noon in May 1996, bright sun. The hills around are scorched orange-brown from drought.*

Bill *is 51,* **Sheila** *is 46,* **Anna** *is 14.* **Bill***, in old gardening shorts and shirt, and a white baseball cap a bit too small, carries a coiled hose and puts it on the lawn.* **Sheila** *comes from the house in a dress with handbag.*

Sheila   Bill? You've left the kettle on – it'll boil dry again.

Bill   I thought you'd gone. Anna's making us tea.

Sheila   In this heat?

Bill   You look nice.

Sheila   Do I?

Bill   You know you do.

Sheila   I never feel I've got it right with Daddy. Whatever I wear, he won't approve.

Bill   – Come here . . . (*for a kiss*)

Sheila   I can't. My shoes will mark the lawn.

Bill   It's had it anyway. Like burnt toast.

Sheila   And you know what he's like – one button loose and he'll notice.

Bill   He's an old man. That frock is wasted on him. You should have worn it last night, for the dinner dance.

Sheila   It's only a tea dress.

Bill   Well, give my regards to Albert. – I put the article for him on the dining table, about the dam in China, did you pick it up?

Sheila   I don't think he's well enough to read.

Slight pause.

The home called this morning –

Bill (*pause*)   Why didn't you tell me?

Sheila (*pause*)   He got a lot worse while you were away, Bill.

Bill (*slight pause*)   Do you want me to come with you?

Sheila   You'll be far away again next week, won't you, there's no point confusing him.

Anna *runs from the house with a skipping rope, in shorts and top.*

Anna   Kettle's boiled – Why are you wearing that awful dress?!

Bill   Anna –

Sheila   I'm going to visit Grandad.

Anna   Can I come?

Sheila   Best not. He's not so good today. Besides you'd need to change, and brush your hair.

Anna   He's not going to die of shock if my hair isn't the way you want.

Sheila   He's not well! Do you understand! He's had a bad turn in the night.

Anna   Okay, don't get at me!

Bill   – Anna! . . . Ring me, if you need.

Sheila   Pray for him.

She starts walking off, to car.

Anna   Mum – give him a big kiss from me.

Bill   Give him my best.

Sheila   Bill, make sure Anna does her chemistry revision.

Exit **Sheila**.

Bill   Where's my cup of tea?

Anna   The milk's turned, so there's no tea. It's the heat.

Bill   Don't tell me it's the heat.

Anna (*starts skipping*)   She shouldn't buy – full fat – it's the fat – that goes off.

Stops to catch her breath.

Bill (*pause*)   Be nice to your Mum. She's upset.

Anna   I can see she's upset! Me being miserable too isn't going to help her, even though you think so.

Anna *skips again while talking*.

Bill   Your irrepressible spirit is too much for her. Do your chemistry.

Anna   – French tomorrow – know it all –

Anna *continues skipping*. **Bill** *uncoils the garden hose to water the lawn*.

Bill   Aren't you a bit old for skipping?

Anna (*stops skipping*)   Aren't you a bit old for shorts?

Bill   Ha ha. Well, you look, you look good in shorts.

Anna   Dad, you're not supposed to use the hose! Because of the water ban.

Bill   I'm not using it am I? I'm unwinding it.

He moves around her.

Anna   A man went to court for watering his tomatoes.

Bill   That's the spirit . . . Look at this lawn.

Anna   It's serious, Dad . . .It's because of the holes in the ozone layer.

Anna *starts skipping again;* **Bill** *unwinds the hose.*

Bill   . . . See if it will reach the runner beans from here.

Anna   Dad – Mind out –

Bill   Haven't you got long legs now. Lovely legs.

Anna (*ignoring him*)   Fourteen . . . fifteen –

Bill   – Which are you?

Anna (*ignoring him*)   – Seventeen . . . eighteen –

Bill   I don't know. I come home from China to find this strange young lady living in my house.

Anna   – Twenty –

Bill   You're sweating. Young ladies aren't supposed to sweat, don't you know that?

Anna (*stops skipping*)   And old men aren't supposed to wear baseball caps.

Bill   You never wear it.

Anna   I do! Dad, I've got to do a hundred.

During the next section, **Anna** *skips again,* **Bill** *attaches one end of the hose to an outside tap.*

Bill   You want to come to the reservoir with me, that'll get your legs moving.

Anna   Skipping – burns – more – calories.

Bill   Spontaneous combustion. On a day like this, you could go up in flames. Bang!

Anna   – Twenty-five – twenty-six – twenty-seven –

Bill Twenty-eight, lay them straight. You're a lucky girl, you've got legs like hers.

Anna – Thirty –

Bill Sixty-two and a half.

Anna (*trips, stops*) – Dad!

Bill That's enough. You'll make a hole in my lawn, elephant.

Anna – You see! Horrible fat wedgy bits.

Bill You want a few curves Annie.

Anna I don't.

Bill You're turning into a fine young lady.

Anna I'm a jelly, look.

Bill Talking of jelly, let's raid the fridge. (*Slight pause.*) Did you hear your Mum in the night? She was cooking.

Anna She likes to get it done at night. When it's cool.

Bill Does she cook at night when I'm away?

Anna She's always cooking. House smells of fried yuck. – I can't skip with you pulling the hose under my feet.

Bill Like a big snake.

Anna I saw an adder by the Post Office.

Bill Hottest May since 1956, they said on the radio.

Anna Dad, don't turn the hose on!

Bill Hey hey, our supply is independent. Thanks to your Grandad.

Anna How come?

Bill How do you think we get water in this house, Annie?

Anna Hadn't thought about it.

Bill   He laid a pipe from the spring in the old village all the way to our house, before he filled the reservoir. – Canny bugger. He could do anything, Albert.

Anna   Poor Grandad. Can hardly lift his hands now.

Bill   He was very good to me, when I was starting out.

Anna   Yes you're always trying to impress him.

Bill   Oh yes?

Anna   – Because he's more famous than you are.

Bill   As if that matters.

Anna   – So you have to go off round the world building bigger and bigger dams, to prove –

Bill   That's enough! (*Slight pause.*) I have nothing to prove.

Anna   Why is Mum frightened of him?

Bill   She's not, Anna. It's – respect. She respects her father, something you could do. (*Pause.*) Now, come to the reservoir with your old Dad.

Anna   I've got to keep skipping. Burn up fat.

Bill   I want to show you – the ruins have appeared, above the water . . . The remains of the old church tower.

Anna   I think the heat's fried your brain.

Bill   Can't believe how much it's dropped, while I've been away. I've not seen the reservoir this low since we worked on the dam.

Anna   Does Grandad know it's drying up?

Bill   It'll fill up again. It'll rain again.

Anna   Might not. Since your lot have messed up the planet.

Bill *goes to the tap, turns it on;* **Anna** *starts to skip again.*

Anna   Might never – ever – rain – again.

Bill   – That's it!

Bill turns the hose on **Anna**, *she grabs the hose and aims it at* **Bill**. *They're laughing and shouting. They don't see* **Sheila** *re-enter the garden.*

Anna   – You're horrible!

Bill   – You asked for it –

Anna   I'll get you –

Bill   Try –

Sheila   Bill!

They are suddenly aware of **Sheila** *and stop.* **Bill** *turns off hose.*

Sheila   What's going on? (*Silence.*) – If anyone walked past our garden . . . !

Bill   . . . What's happened love?

Sheila   I can't . . . go . . .

Bill   Oh love.

Sheila   No – don't – you're all wet – now you've ruined my dress, look!

Anna   I'll get a towel.

Anna *runs off to the house.*

Bill   It's alright – when my parents died I felt –

Sheila   – It's not alright, don't be stupid! It'll never never be alright, ever again. I can't imagine my life without him! (*Rage.*) We've ruined the garden! Look at it – a shambles – brown, shrivelled-up beds – even the wistaria is dying.

Bill   It's not my fault! No rain.

Sheila   You – you – you – you – You didn't see him!

She hits **Bill**'s *chest with her fists.*

Scene Ten: Dew

Garden of **Bill** *and* **Sheila***'s house as in previous scene, but it is present time, 14 July 2012, about 1 a.m. of a stifling hot summer night. Some moonlight.* **Jack** *wears long baggy shorts and no shirt.* **Anna** *wears a white cotton dress which she hasn't done up at the back, and is barefoot.*

Anna   I thought a bird had flown into the window.

Jack   It was a flapjack. Didn't want to break the glass. – It's on the lawn over there.

Anna   Don't leave it or a hedgehog will eat it and have a sugar rush. Ouch. The grass is like a doormat.

Jack   I couldn't sleep.

Anna   Nor me . . .

Faint rumble of thunder.

Jack   It wants to rain. But it can't.

Anna   Can hardly breathe in my room the air is so tight.

Jack   What have you got on?

Anna   I was looking in the cupboards. Found this dress I wore when I was fifteen.

Jack   Yeah it's very – virginal.

Anna   Is it?

Jack   – In a sweet way.

Anna   I'm not sweet now . . . Can you do it up at the back?

Jack   No. I like it like this.

Strokes her naked back instead.

Anna   I'll self-combust if you do that . . .

Jack This afternoon when you walked away across the dam, you didn't look back at me . . . like you were already thinking about someone else.

Anna That's not true! I was thinking about you.

Jack Let me come in the house. You never invite me here.

Anna I like our place on the hill, under the stars.

Jack I want to be with you in your place.

Anna (*hesitates*) They're asleep.

Jack And?

Anna Mum doesn't sleep very well, especially in this heat.

Jack I'll be as quiet as . . . thistledown. (*Pause.*) You don't want me.

Anna Of course I want you . . . I don't think about much else.

Jack But.

Anna Jack it's the room I grew up in . . . And it's only a single bed.

Jack I don't care. I want to hold you all night long.

Anna (*hesitates*) Suppose they wake up, and hear a strange man in the house . . .

Jack Am I a strange man?

Anna You know what I mean.

Look, I just want to respect their place –

Jack Do they respect you?

Anna (*pause*) It never worked, bringing a boyfriend here . . . Always went wrong somehow. And I don't want it to go wrong with us.

Jack I don't want to be your boyfriend.

Silence.

Jack   I want to be with you for the rest of our lives. And they'd better get used to that.

Jack *turns and walks out of the garden.*

Anna   Jack –

Jack   What?

Anna   I'll come with you now.

Jack (*slight pause*)   No.

Anna   I want to.

Jack (*pause*)   Tomorrow morning, before sunrise, meet me up on Edge Moor, by the stone circle. And wear that dress.

Jack *walks away out of sight.* **Anna** *stands in the garden a moment.*

Sheila*'s voice comes from a high-up window.*

Sheila   . . . Anna?

Scene Eleven: Cake

Mid-morning in June 1996, a few weeks after Scene Nine, Skipping.

Anna *is nearly 15 and is in the kitchen, in the white summer dress she was wearing in previous Scene Ten, Dew, and the baseball cap from Scene Nine, Skipping.* **Sheila**, *46, enters in a smart dress and handbag ready to go out, and holds out a postcard to* **Anna**.

Sheila   Postcard from Dad came for you this morning.

Anna   Already? Wow – is that the Yangtze river!

Sheila   – Why are you wearing white?

Anna   You said, at Whitsun everyone used to wear white. I thought Grandad might like it.

Sheila   White makes you look ill.

Anna   You said wear a dress.

Sheila   Let's see the front – oh you need a bra under that.

Anna   Mum! (*Embarrassed.*)

Sheila   Or a cardigan.

Anna   It's boiling.

Sheila   Whitsun is deceptive. (*Checks handbag for keys.*) I was made to wear a white dress and told not to get it dirty. We had to parade through the village to the old well.

Anna   You could talk about that stuff with Grandad. He's better at long ago than – what he had for lunch yesterday.

Sheila   He doesn't remember anything any more.

Anna   He does! It's just – in a different order from us.

Sheila   Last week, he called you Sheila.

Slight pause.

I might as well not bother to come.

Anna   He's your Dad!

Sheila   He prefers you.

Anna   Maybe that's because he thinks I am you.

Sheila   I doubt it, that skirt you had on – he always said I had terrible legs.

Slight pause.

I've run out of things to say to him.

Anna   You don't need to talk, you can just listen.

Sheila   – To you two getting on like a house on fire. That's nice for me.

Anna   Tell him about the Well Dressing you're doing at Landcross this year. How you're making the flower picture.

Sheila   It's only pushing petals into clay, he knows all that.

Anna   He likes to know the tradition is still going.

Sheila   You can tell him.

Anna   I bet he can still remember the names of all the wildflowers.

Sheila   We use shop flowers now, not wildflowers. No one has time to go wandering the hills.

Anna   He taught me the names . . . That's the sort of thing people remember when they've forgotten everything else. (*Pause.*) Must be frightening, knowing you're going to die soon.

Sheila   I don't think he's frightened.

Anna   I do.

No reply from **Sheila**. **Anna** *opens the fridge and takes out a covered bowl of icing, and a cake on a plate.*

Sheila   I hope the fridge isn't de-frosting.

Anna   I made a cake to take with us, for Grandad's birthday.

Sheila   When did you bake that?

Anna   Last night. So it would be cool to ice today.

Sheila   Anna we've got to leave!

Anna   It won't take five minutes. – I'm going to ice it now.

Sheila   Why start on this when we've got to get in the car?

Anna   I've made the icing already, it's in this bowl –

Sheila   Grandad's expecting us at one o'clock sharp. You know he sits and watches the clock, and you know what he's like if we're one minute late.

Anna   – Mum –

Sheila   – Why are you doing this to me?

Anna *is spreading icing on the cake with a spatula.*

Sheila   Stop it –

Anna   – It only takes a moment –

Sheila   You're making a mess of the kitchen. I cleaned everything this morning. – While you were asleep.

Anna   I'll wash up.

Sheila   There won't be time.

Anna   I'll wash up when we get back.

Sheila *grabs the spatula from* **Anna**.

Anna   Mum – don't – now look, icing's gone on my dress.

Sheila   I told you!

Anna   Then let me do it!

Sheila *lets* **Anna** *have the spatula. She quickly finishes icing the cake.*

Sheila   I expect you've had no breakfast.

Slight pause.

Why bother making a cake, you won't eat any, and he won't eat any – only nibble at it.

Anna   There, it's done.

Sheila (*slight pause*)   We can't take that in the car, the icing's not set.

Anna   He might not have another birthday – sorry.

Sheila   You've no idea how hard it is for me. And your Dad being away for months at a time.

Anna   He said he'll be home a bit earlier – by August.

Sheila   That'll be too late.

Anna (*pause*)   I'll hold the cake on my knee in the car.

Sheila (*slight pause*)   I doubt Grandad will remember it's his birthday.

Anna   Doesn't matter. I wanted to make him a cake.

Sheila (*slight pause*)   Come on then, bring it.

Sheila *is going to the back door to exit.*

Anna   Where are the photos?

Sheila   What? Anna we haven't time.

Anna   He asked, last time.

Sheila   Anna –

Anna   He really wanted you to bring some.

Sheila   He took hundreds, I can't go sifting through them all.

Anna   He wanted one of Whitwell . . . You said you'd bring them!

Sheila   I can't remember everything I say to him!

Anna   They'll be in the boxes in the back room –

Sheila   Anna, you get in the car *now*, or you're not coming with me today.

Anna   – You take the cake to the car – I'll run and get the first box I find. – Supposing he dies this week and we hadn't taken them.

Sheila   You're being histrionic now.

Anna *gives the cake to* **Sheila**, *who takes it.* **Anna** *dashes off to the back room.* **Sheila** *looks at the cake. Then she claws out a handful from the middle and throws it on the floor. She pushes the rest of the cake off the plate and on to the floor. A moment.*

Then she kneels down with the plate and scoops some cake back on to the plate. **Anna** *re-enters with an old box of photographs.* **Sheila** *looks up at her.*

Sheila   I slipped. It's these shoes.

Anna   Oh Mum – are you okay?

Sheila   I've spoiled it all now, haven't I.

Anna   No you haven't . . .

Sheila   All your hard work.

Anna   It was fun making it. Can you get up okay?

Sheila   Yes . . .

Anna   You've got icing on your skirt –

Sheila   – Oh no, it'll leave a mark –

Anna   He can't see very well.

Sheila   We could buy another cake on the way there.

Anna   Isn't time.

Sheila   I'm a dreadful mother aren't I.

Anna   No you're not.

Sheila   And a dreadful daughter.

Anna   I'm sure he doesn't think that.

Sheila   You don't know the way he looks at me when you're out of the room. Does my hair look alright?

Anna   I wish Dad was here.

Sheila   Oh fine.

Anna   I just mean – he and I could go instead –

Sheila   You've no idea what your Dad is really like!

Silence.

You know very little about men yet, Anna.

Anna (*pause*)   What do you mean?

Sheila   I'd better phone the home now and say we'll be late.

Blackout.

Scene Twelve: Woundwort

The Anchoress's Cell, 2012, early February, morning. **Catherine** *wanders about her cell as if she can see through the walls to the moor around her.*

Cath   A warm wind is blowing from the tops . . . I'll need to go to Edge Moor for vetch, for binding. Vetch makes a good wreath, canst hoop it round . . . and round . . . and round . . . to fit my head. I must weave the flowers in, then. Jewels of the earth. Christ had a crown of thorns . . . No flowers? I am a bride of Christ. Be not afeared, for the kingdom of heaven is yours . . . – Did you lie with a man? If you did never lie with a man, and you die a maid, you shall be married in death! You shall be a sweet bride in death, crowned with meadow flowers across your brow.

(*She picks flowers.*) Meadowsweet, Eyebright, Crane's Bill, Buttercup, Harebell, Lady's Bedstraw, Campion, Saxifrage, Stitchwort . . . Woundwort . . . Heartsease . . . Forget-me-not.

(*Pause. Calls.*) Father! I wish to make confession! . . . Father? Are you there . . .?

No reply. Lights fade to darkness on **Catherine**.

End of Act One. Interval.

Act Two

Scene One: Cutting

The morning after the end of Act One, Scene Ten: nearly dawn, 14 July 2012. Kitchen in Bill and Sheila's house as before. Sheila in her dressing gown. **Bill** *enters, in his dressing gown.*

Bill Have you been sick again?

Sheila No. A little . . . I came down here so as not to wake you.

Bill Well you have.

Sheila I couldn't sleep at all . . .

Sheila *starts chopping carrots.*

Bill What is it . . .?

Sheila (*swallows*) I was lying there watching the clock, and when it got to three, I thought – it's Anna's birthday now. She's thirty.

Bill *doesn't reply.*

Sheila I look at her, and I think, why is she wasting her life . . .?

Bill *doesn't reply.*

Sheila I keep thinking, what can I do for her?

Bill You've done enough. – Too much, knowing you.

Sheila Have I?

Bill She's been here for weeks. Shall I tell her to go home?

Sheila No – don't do that –

Bill You're not up to it.

Sheila I said she could stay till she finds somewhere to live.

Bill　Doctor Waites said your blood pressure is very high and we have to be extremely careful.

Sheila　I asked him not to tell you.

Bill　Obviously I need to know! We must prioritise your health. – Will you stop chopping.

Sheila　I need to keep busy. So I'm making a shepherd's pie for you and Anna, this evening. We've got a staff meeting and I've got reports to write after school.

Bill　I don't want bloody shepherd's pie. I'm fed up with you making meals you never eat!

Sheila *chops her finger. At this moment* **Anna** *wakes again.*

Sheila　– Damn!

Bill　You've cut yourself?

Sheila　You made me jump. – It's nothing.

Anna *wearily gets out of bed and moves towards the kitchen during:*

Bill　It's bleeding – put it under the tap –

Sheila (*upset*)　No no it's fine. Oh alright.

Sheila *turns the tap on, lets water run over her finger, they quieten.*

Sheila　I just want her to be happy Bill, I really do.

Bill　When I was Anna's age, I couldn't wait to get up and out to work every morning.

Sheila　And I'd be sat here nursing our little girl – she was such a happy baby.

Bill　You did all you could. You're a great mother.

Sheila　I shouldn't have said she can stay . . . Will you tell her?

Bill　Yes. Now back to bed. It's not even dawn.

Sheila　I'm up now. I'll get through the day.

She resumes chopping a carrot.

Bill Get through the day! You're taking the day off.

Sheila I can't possibly. School can't manage without me.

Bill Look at you, you can hardly stand!

Sheila Don't get in a state, Bill –

Bill I'm not! But we don't want a recurrence –

Sheila Don't shout!

Bill Blast, damn this –

Anna *has reached the doorway between the kitchen and the rest of the house by this.*

Sheila I can't cope with this, with you being so tense –

Bill Oh so it's my fault!

Anna (*enters*) Are you alright, Mum?

Sheila Yes of course I'm alright. I'm fine. Happy birthday.

Anna What's up?

Bill It's making your Mum ill, having you here.

Sheila – I didn't say that.

Bill No, she's far too unselfish.

Sheila I know you've got problems, love. I want you to get better.

Bill Why can't you grow up and sort yourself out.

Anna Okay I'll be out of here by tonight.

Sheila No no I didn't mean go now –

Bill – Sheila, you can't cope.

Sheila Of course I can!

Anna It's fine. I'll camp out. I want to stay in the hills.

Sheila You see – Anna can't look after herself –

Anna   I can –

Sheila   No you can't!

Bill   Sheila, will you stop it!

Sheila   – Let's forget about it, forget about all this. It's Anna's birthday! I'm fine now.

Bill *goes at the back door and punches it.*

Bill   – Damn – Blast –

Sheila   Bill! Bill!

Bill   – It won't break! Your father made it so bloody strong.

Anna   Dad, are you okay?

Bill   Do I look it!

Sheila *starts to get breathless.*

Sheila   Don't – Bill!

Anna   Breathe, breathe.

Sheila   He's going to – have a heart attack –

Anna   Don't try and talk Mum.

Slight pause.

I'm not going anywhere.

Sheila   Stay in your room. Stay.

Lights fade on them, as they rise on the hill beyond, where **Jack** *is waiting for* **Anna**, *and we go into next scene.*

Scene Two: Handfast

A short time after previous scene, 14 July 2012. **Jack** *at the crest of Edge Moor. He has woven a wreath of flowers; when he sees* **Anna** *he hides this.*

Anna *wears the same summer dress she wore in Act One, Scene One, Reservoir. Through the scene the light floods the hillside pinky red as the sun rises.*

Anna I ran most of the way up the hill. I could see you standing up here against the sky.

Jack I said meet me before dawn.

Anna Sorry . . . Mum's not well.

Jack Would you rather stay with them?

Anna I'm here. With you.

Jack You're not wearing the dress. I asked you to wear the dress.

Anna I was in a hurry.

Jack It's nearly sunrise. It may be too late.

Anna For what?

Jack . . . Something special.

Anna What . . . ?

Jack For your birthday.

Anna Oh please don't say it's too late.

Jack I wanted us to be at the handfast stone when the morning sun touches it.

Anna The stone circle is turning rosy – let's run –

Jack No, it's your birthday any second now. – Close your eyes.

He takes out a flower wreath and places it on **Anna**'s *head.*

Jack I am yours, for ever, if you are mine . . .

Anna (*takes it off*) What are you doing – no – you can't put that on my head – it's a crant!

Jack – Careful with it –

Anna – It's unlucky.

Jack Unlucky?

Anna When a woman died unmarried, they put a crant on her coffin . . .

Jack   Anna, I made this for you, to marry me! – At the handfast stone. I want to join hands through the hole in the stone, and make our vow, like people did long, long ago.

Anna (*long pause*)   Not yet.

Jack   What?

Anna   I'm not, – I'm not ready.

(*Pause.*) It's a beautiful idea.

Jack   Don't patronise me.

Anna   I'm sorry, don't be –

Jack   – What is it that's not good enough, about me?

Anna   I didn't say that.

Jack   That's what I'm getting.

Anna   It's not you, it's me – I want to get sorted out . . . first.

Jack   I love you as you are.

Anna (*slight pause*)   I'm being stupid. You're so lovely.

Jack   But . . . You don't love me as much as I love you.

Anna   No! – I – (*Hesitates.*).

Jack   You don't. Be honest.

Anna   – I do!

Jack   Not like – if you left me, – it would be the end of the world.

Anna   I do . . . I find it hard to say . . .

Jack   It's all about your feelings, never about mine.

Anna   Jack. I didn't say no, I said –

Jack   – When it suits you. (*Pause.*) Okay, well the moment's gone.

Anna (*sighs, picks up the wreath*)   Will this keep? You've woven it so beautifully.

Jack . . . I wanted you to be happy, and do all the things you said you wanted.

Anna I've fucked it up. Haven't I. (*Pause.*) Please – (*Stops.*)

Jack (*slight pause*) I'm not sure, now.

Maybe the moment will come back, maybe it won't.

Anna Don't say that.

Jack Why not? You've been saying it.

Let's see how it goes.

Long pause.

Anna The sun's up – the reservoir's burning red.

Jack It's dying.

Anna There's some men down there – on the mud.

– At the side of the dam . . . Jack, do you see?

Jack (*pause*) They're opening the sluice gates.

Anna – Why?

Jack The level's so low, they've decided to drain off the useable water, and store it in another reservoir further down the valleys.

Anna How long will it take?

Jack (*slight pause*) I don't know . . . a week.

Anna And then we'll see what's down there.

The bones of the village.

The dawn light fades, the gloom of the Anchoress's Cell is filled with the same light coming through the outside window as we go into next scene.

Scene Three: Floodgates

The Anchoress's Cell, February 1212. **Priest** *is at the interior window between the interior of the church and the cell. The red light of sunrise falls across the cell to* **Catherine** *kneeling.*

Cath   Father –

Priest   Catherine?

Cath *stops her mouth with her fist; she is choking and can't breathe.*

Cath (*hesitates*)   I want to make confession.

. . . 'Tis a kind of hell inside me.

Priest (*pause*)   Often times the devil comes to a woman alone, whose mind is unclean. He uses her as a privy, and empties foul thoughts down her throat . . . Then her soul will swell with malice – and see evil intent in a man where there is no proof! . . .It is for God alone to make judgment.

Slight pause.

Dost thou wish to confess?

Cath   Nay, now I fear to speak . . .

Priest   Close the floodgates of thy mouth and dam up thy foul thoughts, and these will drown in the poisonous wrath of thy body.

Cath   There's such a boiling and chunnering inside me!

– What can I do?

Priest   Keep the shutter to the outside world closed, from now on.

Slight pause.

Thou must fast for seven days and nights.

We will starve out the Serpents of Evil.

Cath   O God, strip off all my flesh that feeds these beasts. I'd scour out my mouth with thorns, and put leeches on my tongue to suck me dry . . .

Priest If thou truly repent –

Cath I do!

Priest Then Our Father will send thee suffering, to purge thy mortal sins.

Cath (*tries to smother the retching sounds*) Uh uh uh uh uh . . .

Priest Our Lady Mary, who is the model for all women, spoke so little that her words are recorded but four times in the scriptures.

Cath Mmm . . . (*Gagging herself with her fist.*)

Priest In silence shall be thy strength.

Lights fade on them as we go into next scene.

Scene Four: Night Mummy

The bedroom, late in the night of 14 July 2012, after Act 2, Scene Two, Handfast. The room is lit by moonlight coming through the window. **Anna** *is in bed, lying still but not asleep. We see she has the flower wreath beside her.* **Sheila** *enters.*

Sheila Mummy?

Anna . . . Mum?

Pause.

Sheila . . . Where's Mummy?

Pause.

Sheila I need Mummy . . .

Anna (*hesitates*) It's alright . . . You're safe.

Sheila Is that Mummy?

Anna *lets out a deep breath.*

Anna Yes, it's Mummy . . . Mummy's here.

Sheila *lets out a sobbing breath, and moves towards* **Anna**, *who puts her arms out to hold her.*

Blackout.

Scene Five: Slut

The reservoir, a few days after previous scene, July 2012. **Anna** *joins* **Jack** *on the expanse of mud beside the small amount of remaining water. Early evening, the light is sultry.*

Anna   Sorry I'm late.

Jack   I thought you weren't coming.

Anna   I said I'd come today.

Jack   It's a kind of bullying, this thing you're doing now – coming some days and not others.

Anna   Is it? It isn't meant to be.

Jack   And you're wearing the dress.

Anna   Yes.

Jack   We're going to wade into the water – it's muddy – why the fuck are you wearing that?

Anna   Because it's the special moment – going to find the well stone.

Jack   Yeah well it's deeper than I thought, the last pool. It's below the level of the sluice gates, so it won't ever dry up – unless they bring some machine and pump it out. But they won't, the mud's too soft.

Anna   Then it must be where the spring comes up.

Jack   Well done.

Anna   And there's the pipe that supplies our house.

Jack   You don't need me, do you.

Anna   Of course I do! We're doing this together.

I don't know where the well stone is . . . Can you see down through the water?

Jack   I expect you'll find it. You can go and make your own map.

Anna   Jack . . .

Jack If you think the stone is down there, why don't you get some flowers and make a picture and do a well dressing? Do a nice little flower arranging festival. In your nice dress.

And then go home to Mummy and Daddy.

Anna You know I want to find something more truthful than that.

Something ancient and eternal.

Jack Do you?

Anna Yes.

Jack I need a real woman for that.

Anna (*takes a breath*) What's up?

Jack Oh you've noticed.

Anna Is it something I've done?

Jack You're changing. Your face is really different.

Anna Is it? I feel so much better.

Jack How nice for you.

Slight pause.

And I feel more and more uneasy when I'm with you.

Anna Why?

Jack I think it's best not to say . . .

Anna – Why?

Jack Because I love you. (*Pause.*) Do you believe that?

Anna Yes yes I do.

Jack So I can't tell you . . .

Anna Please tell me. I want to know.

Jack I think what's inside you, is really evil.

Anna How?

Jack   After we make love – you talk in your sleep.

. . . But not in your own voice.

Anna   Like – who?

Jack   I don't know. Something – violent.

Anna   But I feel so much happier, with you.

Jack   That's bollocks.

Anna   I love you.

Jack (*long pause*)   I can't trust you.

Anna   I do!

Jack   No, you want to use me, and what's in you wants to screw me up.

Anna   That's horrible –

Jack   I should've trusted my instincts from the beginning.

Anna   What instincts – you said you could heal this –

Jack   I can't heal you, Anna. Even though I love you so much.

Anna   You said you're happier with me than you've ever been –

Jack   I didn't want to frighten you.

Anna   You said we'd get it out.

Expels all her breath in a sound between a retch and a roar.

Jack   Stop it!

Anna   Jack –

Jack   – Stop dumping all your shit on me!

Anna   I'm not. Am I?

Jack   It makes me so wound up being near you.

That's what you do to men, isn't it.

Anna No!

Jack You said none of your relationships ever work out, and that it's your fault.

Anna I want this to work. I want to love you.

Jack Do you?

Anna Yes.

Jack (*pause*) I don't think you're capable of love.

Anna Uh –

Jack . . . I think you only know how to provoke.

Anna I – how?

Jack Like – that dress. Teasing me. Flaunting yourself.

Anna I thought you liked this dress. You said it's sexy.

Jack So that's why you're wearing it – to turn me on.

Anna I want to feel sexy.

Jack I can see that.

Anna . . . And I like sex.

Jack I know you do . . . But you can't see what's happening to you. It's slutty . . . whoreish.

YOU LOOK LIKE A SLUT.

Anna You wanted –

Jack DON'T TELL ME WHAT I WANT!

You don't know me, you don't know me at all!

Anna I'm sorry.

Jack You're not sorry. I'm going.

Anna No –

Jack I can't take any more of this.

Anna Please, Jack –

Jack   You make me sick.

Anna   – Wait –

Jack   Let go! LET GO!

Anna   I'm sorry, I'm sorry –

Jack   You're not.

Anna   I am.

Jack   Get down on your knees.

Anna (*kneels*)   I'm really sorry.

Slight pause. **Anna** *goes to open his fly, but she can't, and turns her head away.* **Jack** *turns her face back to his crotch.*

Jack   Go on.

Silence.

Anna   Not now –

Jack   – I SAID!

Anna   – Later, when we're –

Jack   See? You don't care about me, what I need.

Anna   Jack –

Jack   You wind me up, wind me up, wind me up –

Anna   I –

Jack   You don't think I'm good enough – you look at me in your patronising way – you think you'll play along with this whole thing and then dump me when you've had enough, you don't really care about me, or anything, because you're locked into your own mad version of who you are and you're never, ever, going to be able to love anyone, you're so fucked up.

Silence.

Jack   Go on, cry.

Anna   – I'm not crying.

She is taking big breaths.

Jack You are – and you think I'll hug you and make it better –

Anna I'm not – I'm – sorry.

Jack Yes I should think so.

Anna – I'm sorry I'm sorry –

Jack You're not.

Anna I am! I'm sorry sorry sorry sorry sorry.

She prostrates herself on the ground at his feet.

Anna I'm so sorry, I'm wrong I'm bad I'm useless – Sorry isn't good enough, I know – What do you want me to say?

Bangs her head on the ground.

Anna I'm so bad, I'm so wrong, so bad – so wrong – worthless.

Jack Jesus. You're mad.

Anna Please forgive me.

Jack Don't you touch me!

Anna – Please forgive me, please say you forgive me.

Jack – I said don't touch me!

Anna – Don't go!

Jack You hit me! I could get really angry now. I could get really angry.

Anna – I didn't hit you.

Jack – You don't EVER HIT a man.

Blackout.

Scene Six: Black Hole

The kitchen of the house, a short time after the previous scene, 14 July 2012, evening. **Sheila** *is in the kitchen at the sink.*

Sheila (*calls*)   Bill. Do you want tomatoes in the salad? Or separate?

Anna *bangs on the back door.*

Sheila   Come in.

Anna   – Open the door!

Sheila   I've got my hands full. It's not locked.

Anna *enters, very shaky.*

Sheila   What's happened to you?

Anna   I don't know.

Sheila   What've you done?

Anna (*makes a noise of hurting*)

Sheila   Sssh – Oh poor Anna –

Anna   Don't –

Sheila   I'm trying to help, love.

Anna   I'm stupid. I'm so stupid.

Sheila   Come here –

Anna   No don't touch me I'm not worth hugging.

Sheila   Oh dear dear dear you are in a state.

(*Calls.*) Bill!

Tell me what's happened.

Anna   I've messed up again.

Sheila   It can't be that bad.

Anna   It is.

Sheila   You're not in a good state at the moment, whatever it is will be better tomorrow.

Anna It won't be. Not this time. This time I see –

Sheila – See what?

Anna How horrible I am.

Sheila Don't say that!

Anna I'm completely fucking useless.

Sheila That's a dreadful thing to say.

Anna I am. I'm horrible, that's why no one wants to be with me.

Sheila Anna, pull yourself together.

Anna Don't you ever feel – you're so crap – what's the point?

Whatever I do – I can't escape being me? That's the problem – I'm the problem.

Sheila Yes sometimes I feel very low. Very low indeed. I've never told you or your Dad how bad.

Slight pause.

I say to myself, come on Sheila, make yourself useful. So I go out and keep busy, deliver the parish newsletter. And I get through it.

Anna But I can't.

Sheila You can.

Anna I can't!

Sheila Don't shout!

Anna Uh – uh, uh –

Bill *enters.*

Bill What's going on?

Sheila I don't know what to do, Bill.

Bill What's happened – Anna, what's up?

Anna   Uh uh.

Sheila   She's having a breakdown –

Bill   I'll call the doctor.

Anna   – No, don't, I don't want to see anyone.

Bill   Ah so you can talk.

Anna   Dad – uh uh – Dad –

Bill   Oh Annie love –

Sheila (*crying*)   Oh I can't bear it –

Bill   It's alright Sheila.

Sheila   It's not alright. I'm scared.

Bill   Come on now. Deep breaths. – Anna.

Anna   – Doesn't matter.

Bill   Anna –

Anna   You look after her. I'll go.

Bill   Don't go –

Anna   Yes. Better. Get out the way.

Anna *exits*.

Sheila   – I'm shaking all over.

Bill   It's shock. We've all had a fright. Probably the heat, feels like a storm's due.

Sheila   Where are you going –

Bill   I'm not, I'm just looking to see where Anna's gone – She needs help –

Sheila   I need help! I need help!

Bill   Hey –

Sheila *starts choking and panting*.

Bill   Now there's no need for that –

Sheila   Don't touch me! Get away – You're useless.

Sheila *exits as the lights fade on kitchen, she goes to the bedroom and gets into bed.* **Bill** *remains in the kitchen a moment then follows.*

Scene Seven: Warrior Sequence

The present, July 2012 immediately after the previous scene, intercuts with February 2012 in the cell. In the present we move between the bedroom of the house, where **Sheila** *is in bed, and the reservoir, to which* **Anna** *is going. The daylight is draining from the land throughout the scene, in the present time and in the cell.*

Bedroom: **Sheila** *has shut the door,* **Bill** *is outside:*

Bill   Sheila? Can you hear me? (*Knocks.*) Sheila. . . let me in . . .

I'm sorry. Whatever I've done.

Sheila *slowly and deliberately arranges the quilt on the single bed into a perfectly aligned position. Then she gets back into bed, trying not to disturb the covers. With tiny slow gestures she begins to smooth the covers. She mumbles at first.*

Sheila   Quilt pillow and blanket. Blanket, pillow and quilt. Quilt pillow and blanket. Blanket, pillow and quilt. You will lie there, you will lie there, you will lie there.

Continues below.

Lights up on the cell, where **Catherine** *hurls herself about, pinching and grabbing her own flesh.*

Sheila   No don't do that. Do you hear me? Stay there pillow like I put you. And blanket, will you lie straight please. Yes. With the edge exactly across here. I said – (*Stops.*) Blanket. (*Pause.*) Right now I'm giving you one more chance, all of you, pillow blanket and quilt. Quilt if you slip off I am not going to pick you up off the floor, no you can just lie there all night, no I'm not even going to look at you. No I'm not. I don't care. Now blanket, I'm giving you one chance to behave – I'll pull the edge up to my mouth. I said – oh! Don't then, don't lie straight. Ever ever ever. See if I care! And now – oooh, pillow, I know you are slipping down my back, trying to get away, ha ha ha, I can feel you. I've got you. Yes little pillow, you stupid little pillow, I am not impressed. Because you are, you know what you are, a stupid stupid, little – CUNT pillow – you know what you are? You are for BEATING! Squash – you – down – fuck YOU! Fuck YOU! – You look at me like that, I will just have to HIT you!

Sheila *falls back, shocked by her frenzy. She listens to her own wild breathing. In the cell.*

Cath (*speaks with a deeper voice*)   You made me do that. You made me do that, for your flesh is weak, your flesh is temptation.

Priest *is at the closed inner window to the church.*

Priest   Catherine, I heard thee speak . . .

Cath   . . . I spoke? (*Afraid.*) How did I speak?

Priest   Thou spake as a man.

Cath   I am possessed by the devil!

Puts her fist in her mouth.

Priest   I did not hear the devil. I heard – a man.

Cath   Nay – Forgive me father.

Priest   Open the shutter – I bring water, take it and drink.

Cath   Nay.

Priest *starts banging on the shutter.*

Priest   I beseech thee, open the shutter –

Cath   Nay!

Priest   Thou must eat and drink now! – Fast no more.

Cath   I do not deserve to have flesh. I will scrape and scour this flesh off this body, you will not see me then. The Devil cannot find me then.

Priest   Thou hast fasted long enough.

(*Hesitates.*) – The Bishop orders thee to eat.

Cath   Nay. Our Father has sent me sweet suffering.

Already a torrent fills me . . .

This pain is sent to wash away all my father's sins.

Priest   What sins?

Cath   O I am a girt sinner, to suffer this much.

Priest   – What sins? Sister, open the shutter.

Cath   This is my tomb, alone.

Priest *forces open the shutter.*

Priest   – Then I will enter and hold the cup to thy lips.

Cath   You are forbidden to enter!

Priest   I cannot let thee suffer more.

Cath   No man may enter my cell, not e'en the Priest, you told me!

Priest   Aye. . .Then I am no longer a Priest – if a Priest is one who would leave thee to die alone.

He puts all his strength on the edging stone below the church window and heaves at it. In the bedroom **Sheila** *is seeing the same wall stones fall.*

Sheila   Bill, Bill! The wall is opening –

The wall is falling. The sky is falling.

In the cell.

Cath   Look not upon my flesh! My flesh is sin.

Priest   Take this cup and drink.

Cath   I see the rock . . .

Priest   . . . The rock of the Tomb?

Cath   The girt rock by the well . . .

Priest   Speak. I am listening.

Cath   . . . Before me now, the girt big stone. All the hills around, buried in white. Snowing fast. I run to the stone, for that's where the sheep hide. The moon hanging and the village asleep, drowning int' white.

Anna *is near the reservoir, she speaks breathless from running. The light is draining fast from the land.*

Anna   You go out the back of our house, through the gap in the wall, and down below is water, white, shining – as if the sky has fallen down. (*Stops.*) But it's gone. No water any more.

In the cell, there is a brighter patch of evening sun left.

Cath   (*breathes hard*) Not a sound int' village, tho' he comes after me . . . Our breath freezing ont' air, my father says, woah there, let me catch up with thee . . . But I'm faster –

(*Breathes hard.*) Uh-uh-uh –

Anna   – And then you jump, on to the mud – and run, run all the way across the mud, through the walls, broken walls, empty windows, watching me – I don't care, you can't stop me now.

Cath   I'm at the stone. There's nowhere to hide. E'en the hawthorn that grows from the rock has not a leaf on her. And sheep quaking int' shelter of the rock, for the snow is blowing.

Anna   Scraps of water between the ruins – not enough – where is it – where is it – the deep pool that won't dry up –

Cath   My father comes.

Anna   Here it is, here it is – (*Calms herself.*)

The pool is still and deep black. I can slip in now . . .

Anna *gets into the water soundlessly and disappears.*

The last of the evening sun lights **Catherine***.*

Cath   He holds me tight, he says – thou'rt like a lamb that struggles when it receives the brand, and I mun hold thee hard.

He says – thou leadest me into temptation. Thou art wicked.

(*Pause.*) I looked not for shame, but down . . . and there was blood opening ont' snow like roses.

Pause.

See, how I am damned. How I led him into temptation.

Priest   You have confessed, and your father is forgiven.

Cath   His soul is saved?

Priest   His soul is saved. You have done penance enough.

Cath   Thanks be to God.

Priest   Eat I pray thee, take this bread . . . One piece?

Cath   Nay – now I will leave this place for I am damned.

Priest   Catherine . . .

Cath   I'd sooner you and all the village stoned me, for then at least I'd die punished, and have some chance of seeking heaven.

Priest (*thinks*)   I will find another way.

Cath   There is no other way. It is written, and you have told me these past months: it is God's law.

Priest   God is merciful to all living creatures, even the sparrow on the tree.

Cath   But not to a woman who has led a man into temptation.

In the bedroom: **Sheila** *pulls out a small dusty box from among the stones of the wall. In the cell.*

Cath   Why do you weep?

Priest   I feared you had gone away.

Cath   Not yet.

Priest   . . . Will you sip this water?

Cath   Nay, I am pure now. No flesh to weigh me to earth.

Priest   See how the evening sun comes in the cell.

Cath   I cannot lift my head, my eyes are on the light beyond this world.

Priest   So cold . . . let the sun warm you.

Cath   Light can shine through me. And the pure white light burns inside me now . . . I need only my bones, my bones are the lantern sides to hold the flame of the spirit.

Priest   Open your hands – they are stiff from prayer.

Cath   See how the light shines through them. Leaf hands.
    And my arms are scoured clean,
    And my legs are withered,
    As the tree in winter.
    Cold black the furrows
    Between my ribs.
    There is no dawn in me.
    Chill wind my breath,
    Rattling my ribs.
    All is still
    All is quiet.
    I am nowt.

Priest   Open your mouth Catherine.

Cath (*refuses – makes a sound*)

Priest Open your mouth. You must take water.

Cath (*animated*) Eve opened her mouth and bit the flesh of
the apple.
  Where's my mouth?
  Above or below?
  Both!
  Gaping wide and red.
  A wound I cannot heal.
  Even though I speak not, I cannot close it.
  Even though I eat not, I cannot starve it off me.
  For it goes right through me.
  See, how a woman is undone from the beginning,
  For having a mouth.

*In the bedroom the golden light of sunset is spreading across the
floor:*

Sheila The walls are leaking. The floor is shining with light
. . .

Cath I can see it now.
  The great shining water.
  It's coming –
  Faster than horses,
  Stronger than the wind,
  Taller than the church,
  Louder than storms,
  Bigger than hate,
  Death is too bright!
  Father, I did not know
  There was this passion in the world,
  And now it is too late.

Silence.

Priest (*quietly*) Lord receive this your child Catherine.

– Father have mercy on her!

Priest *continues to pray fast under his breath during the following, sprinkling her with holy water. Light ripples like water, as* **Priest** *lays* **Catherine**'s *hands across her body.*

Cath   The sea is moving in to me.
   The water is in me and the water is all around me.
   I am everything and nothing.

Priest *closes* **Catherine**'s *eyes.*

Priest   Father forgive me.

Sound of waves as we travel into Scene Eight, Underwater.

Scene Eight: Underwater

Deep cold water, under the reservoir. **Anna** *drifts down,* **Catherine** *is there. This is a dance which becomes a fight.*

Cath   Hello.

Anna   Hello? Who's there?

Cath   'Who's there?' Thou knowest.

Anna   Is it you?

Cath   Aye.

Anna   Where?

Cath   Behind thee.

Anna   You're small.

Cath   Let me see thy teeth – look how white, and all in a row.

Anna   You're cold.

Cath   Aye. 'Tis cold down here.

Anna   You're so cold.

Cath   Been cold a long time.

Anna   Did you know I was coming?

Cath (*slight pause*)   Hoped not. Been praying for thee.

Anna   Why? Did you want me?

Cath   Yes and no. Didn't want thee coming down here.

Anna   Why?

Cath   It is without end.

Anna   It's beautiful.

Cath   The water cares not for thee.

Anna   I want to be water. It's easy.

Cath   No.

Anna   I'm as big as the sea.

Cath   Thou wilt have to swim back.

Anna   I'm too weary.

Cath   Kick thy legs. Quicken!

Anna   I can't . . .

Cath   Go! Go on, thou munst.

Anna   Why?

Cath   Because I cannot! I did not!

Anna   I've finished there.

Cath   No.

Anna   There's nothing more I can do.

Cath   There is . . .

Anna   I don't want to leave you! I'm scared.

Cath   I was scared.

Anna   And now?

Cath   I'm nothing.

Lights change, darkness becomes daybreak as **Anna** *surfaces from the water and drags herself out, muddy and wet. A few drops of rain fall.* **Anna** *puts out her hands.*

Anna   It's raining.

As **Anna** *returns to the house, the daylight comes up but rain builds to torrential downpour. The whole landscape becomes rain.*

Scene Nine: Flood

The kitchen of the house. July 2012, a short time after we saw **Anna** *at the end of the previous scene. Outside, rain obscures all the views.*

Bill *enters through the back door, in a well-worn sou'wester and mackintosh, carrying a bedraggled remnant of a tomato plant in a pot. He is dripping rain. He puts down the plant and takes off the wet outerwear as he talks to the plant.*

Bill   Poor tomatoes.

Battered to death by rain.

What a summer.

– You are the last survivor.

So don't give up on me eh.

Good job I redug the storm drain in June.

– Ha, she said I was barmy.

Now it's swirling around like the mouth of hell.

(*Calls to bedroom.*) Sheila . . .? Want a brew?

Silence except for rain.

Well I do. (*Opens fridge door, no light.*) Aha, the power is off.

(*Calls.*) Sheila, the power is off now, don't turn on any lights.

Water trickles down the wall from above the sink.

Oh hello. Where's that coming from?

Bill *examines the trickle of water coming down the wall above the sink, tries to stop it.*

. . . Gutters must be overflowing.

(*Looks out of window.*) Can't see a thing out there.

. . . You should be careful what you wish for.

Anna *opens back door and steps into kitchen in the white dress, torn and muddy and wet, closes the door quickly on the rain.*

Anna　Hi Dad.

Bill　And where have you been?

Anna　You know me. I had to get out.

Bill　All night. You had me worried.

Anna　– It was a warm night.

Bill　Till the heavens broke. You didn't have your tent.

Anna　I was fine.

Beat.

It's brilliant, isn't it!

Bill　The rain can't get into the ground, because it's hard as concrete.

(*Of water coming down wall above sink.*) And look at this . . .

Anna　Where's that coming from?

Bill　What the insurance people call an Act of God, so I'll be getting nothing back, for all my down payments.

Anna　Is it that bad?

Bill　Roof's leaking upstairs. We're approaching emergency levels, Anna. I've got buckets in the loft.

– No don't touch that tap!

Anna　– Just want a drink –

Bill I said don't! Now look –

Tap is now trickling and won't turn off.

Anna Sorry – it won't –

Bill That tap won't stop now. It's the same upstairs. The water pressure's gone ballistic. The spring must be disgorging ten times its usual output.

Anna Really – the spring?

Bill This house is flooding from the inside out.

Anna It's not the end of the world. Where's Mum?

Bill In bed. In your bedroom. – No don't go in, Anna. She needs her rest. Been a bit out of sorts.

Anna You don't look too good.

Bill I'll go and check the bath taps aren't starting.

You stay here and watch the sink.

Bill *exits into the house.*

Sheila *enters from the bedroom, carrying a smallish old silk-covered box.*

Sheila What have you done!

Anna Something so amazing – you wouldn't believe it . . .

Sheila You've dirtied your dress!

Anna It is raining . . .

Sheila You naughty girl.

Anna . . . No, I'm not.

Sheila You are! You're a bad girl!

Anna Mum –?!

Sheila The lace is torn right off the hem –!

Anna Is it –?

Sheila Where have you been? . . . Sheila?

Anna Down to the – Where do you think . . .?

Sheila . . . To the well stone? By yourself?

Anna Yes.

Sheila I told you not to!

Anna . . . Why?

Sheila You know why.

Anna (*guessing*) . . . Someone else was there . . .?

Sheila – Who was there?

Anna (*copying*) Who was there . . .?

(*Slight pause.*) Someone . . . you know?

Sheila Yes.

Anna Who was it?

Sheila Can't say.

Anna Tell me.

Sheila Mustn't.

Anna (*takes a breath*) Sheila, tell me who was there.

Sheila Father said I mustn't! Or something terrible will happen and I'll never see him again!

Anna Did he?

Sheila Yes! He said you'll sew the lace back on my dress, and no one will ever know.

Anna . . . Will I?

Sheila Will you Mummy?

Anna . . . I'll try.

Sheila I'll put the lace in my jewellery box, to keep safe.

Bill *re-enters from the house.*

Bill The back wall is cracked, subsidence – no one go in the back bedroom.

Anna   Ssh Dad –

Bill   What's going on?

Anna   Someone's hurt . . .

Bill   Sheila? Are you alright?

Sheila   Yes. Yes. (*She stands up.*)
  – See me!
  In my new white frock for Whitsun.
  I'm a giant.
  Here I come down the path bam BAM squashing all the
  ant people with my sandals.
  He's coming. – Don't – can't you see I'm a giant?
  I'm going to run. Running.
  I'm SO BRAVE!
  Run run run run RUN.
  I HAVE to run. You're making me.
  Or I'll get a good hiding.
  What's a good hiding?
  Run run run run RUN the long grass. All tickly on my
  arms.

Out of breath.

  Look at the wall! Blue black stones.
  Blue black. PUSH.
  Blue black all fall down. Brave me.

Breath as in running.

  Blue black blue black blue black blue black
  Blublakblu – uh – blakblu, blakblublakblublakblublakblu –
  – Hate this dress – too tight – across my front
  – where I breathe . . .
  Don't catch me Daddy can't you see how brave I am can't
  you see I'm a GIANT.
  I'll – go – behind – the rock! . . . The big rock.

She is catching her breath.

  Hiding, a good hiding.

Breath calming. Then suddenly.

– NO DADDY NO!
Don't.
Please don't.
I'll be good.
– Can't you see, I'm a giant!
No no no no no no no no no no . . .

Silence.

Anna Sheila, get the piece of lace from your jewellery box and I'll see if I can mend your dress.

Sheila (*shakes her head*) Mmm mmm.

Anna Please.

Sheila Mustn't open it.

Anna I can help you –

Sheila – Mustn't!

Anna Why . . .?

Sheila Because of the photographs.

Anna What photographs?

Sheila *opens the lid of the box.*

Sheila Those ones . . .

Bill . . . What are they?

Sheila You know.

Anna No, I don't know.

Sheila The bad ones – you mustn't look.

Anna . . . Why.

Bill *looks through the photos as* **Sheila** *speaks.*

Sheila Because – I'm doing a bad thing. A very very bad thing. Wicked.

And if anyone sees they'll know I'm a wicked dirty little girl for doing . . .

Bill   Oh God . . .

Sheila   Shouldn't wear that dress. Daddy couldn't help it.

Bill   Anna –

Anna   I know. I know.

Sheila   I'm hiding them in here – in the secret underneath tray so no one will ever see them. And Daddy will help me hide them in our secret place. Then no one else can find them.

Pause.

But God sees everything, doesn't he?

He knows I'm wicked now.

A flash of lightning. Water from outside starts to spread from the door sill across the floor.

Sheila (*terrified*)   He's seen me!

Bill   Now what – the storm drain must be overflowing –

Bill *grabs his coat and opens the door, dashes outside, shutting the door behind him. A crack of thunder overhead.*

Sheila   No . . .! I'm sorry, Father I'm sorry.

A rumble. The room darkens, rain comes on even stronger.

Sheila   Now he's coming to get me.

Anna   Don't be frightened.

Sheila   You don't know what might happen!

Anna   No, I don't.

A flash of lightning.

Sheila   – There he is . . .!

She sees her Dad in the room.

Anna   Where?

Sheila   . . . Waiting for me.

Anna   Yes, I see him . . .

Sheila   No no no –

Anna   He can't hurt you any more. – Tell him that.

Sheila (*pause*)   I can't.

Anna   I see you. I see you, Grandad.

And I know what you've done.

Sheila   Don't tell – God will punish you!

Anna   God is love. Love is in the room.

Sheila   Daddy's moving nearer!

Anna   Look, he's only a sad man.

Sheila   Is he?

Anna   Look how scared he is.

Sheila   Is he?

Anna   Yes. (*To the Grandad.*) Is there anything you want
to say?

Silence except for rain.

Sheila   Is he sorry . . .

Anna   Ask him.

Sheila *can't say it.*

Anna   Ask him. Sheila.

Sheila   . . . Are you sorry? For – for . . .

Anna   – What you've done to her?

Silence for a moment.

Sheila   I can see who's behind him! . . . And – I can see who's behind him . . . And –

Anna   Stop. You can't ever see the beginning.

It goes back and back into the dark.

But we can see the end.

Sheila   Where?

Anna   Here. Now.

The rain stops, a break of light in the clouds lightens the room from now. **Bill** *opens the back door and comes in, dripping wet.*

Bill   There are waterfalls – above us – the hillside is streaming. The back garden is filling with water.

Sheila   Hello Bill.

Bill   – What?

Sheila   You came here – and saw me – and married me.

Anna   Dad . . . (*Encouraging him.*)

Bill   Yes love, I married you – because . . . you're the girl I love.

Sheila   Bill . . . What do we do now? Tell me what to do.

Bill   I don't know.

Anna (*quietly*)   . . . The garden is filling with water?

Bill (*quietly*)   The moors are so dry the rain is running straight off and down to the reservoir. Only – this house is in the way.

Anna   Mum.

Sheila   Hmm?

Anna   Go and get your coat on.

Sheila   No I don't think so.

Anna *runs into house to get coats.*

Sheila Are we going somewhere?

Bill Yes – we're – Going to somewhere new . . .

Sheila I'd better get some overnight things then.

Bill No love. Don't worry about that.

Anna *re-enters with coats for her and* **Sheila**.

Bill We've got about two minutes.

Anna What else do we need?

Bill Passports. The spare cash.

Bill *opens the fridge and reaches to the back, gets out a Tupperware box.*

Sheila *is putting her coat on.*

Anna I thought that was Wensleydale . . . What about
– (*She stops.*)

Bill – Photos . . . Oh Jesus.

Anna Don't crack yet Dad, come on.

Rumbling noise of floodwater starts on hill, grows through next lines.

Bill – There's a drawing of yours – in my study upstairs –
you did when you were little.

Anna I'll do you another one.

Sheila I'm ready!

Anna *moves to open the back door.*

Sheila – Sounds like the sea out there.

Anna It does, doesn't it. Come on, let's go.

She opens the back door. Ahead on the hill she and **Bill** *can see the run-off approaching.*

Bill . . . It's a wall coming down the hill – only it's water.

Sheila   – Ooh –

Anna   You take her first, Dad.

Bill (*helping* **Sheila**)   Come on love.

Quick sticks. Round the side to the car.

Bill *and* **Sheila** *move out of sight. The floodwater sounds are growing louder.* **Anna** *stands looking round the room for a moment.*

A whoosh of water spray comes through an open window.

She goes to the door and opens it wide.

Anna   Let the sky fill the house.

Anna *steps out of the house, leaving the door wide open. She throws down the house key, then turns and runs away, as the storm grows, the sound of water rushes nearer and the sky darkens to night.*

Blackout.

Scene Ten: Ruins

The garden of the house a week after previous, late July 2012.

Lights slowly rise for a summer's day, sheep call not far off. We see a part of the house wall and garden. The storm-damaged back door is lying on the ground. **Anna** *watches.* **Bill** *is swinging an axe into the door.*

Bill   You – brute, Albert.

Stops for a moment.

Some days I want to kill him.

Other days I'm exhausted.

. . . I had absolute faith in him.

Anna   Don't blame yourself.

Bill   He lied. He said the house would never flood.

Anna   Water will always find a way through.

Bill That's very true.

Anna You told me that. When I was small and you were explaining hydraulics to me.

Bill Did I? So I have said some useful things to you in life . . .

Anna Just the one.

Bill (*gives the axe to* **Anna**) Your turn – Do you know how to do it?

Anna Dad, I've used an axe before.

Bill Okay.

Anna *swings the axe into the wood and splits a panel of the door.*

Anna Let's get every single thing in the house that he made, and smash them up. – The rocking chair . . .

Bill – The hall table. The bread bin . . . My desk!

Anna The jewellery box – I destroyed that already.

Bill (*upset now*) Of all the people in the world to hurt – your own little girl.

Anna It may have been done to him, when he was little.

Bill That's no excuse, is it! (*Pause.*) My father hit us, but I've never hit you, have I?

Bill *takes the axe and has another chop at the door.*

Anna (*pause*) You said things that knocked me down.

Bill Well . . . It's toughened you up.

Anna No, it hurt.

Anna *takes the axe and swings it into the wood. Then.*

Anna Now the back door has gone, do I still owe you three pounds twenty-five for the key?

Bill (*pause*)   There are times when . . . you know you're not behaving right . . . you know you're taking it out on someone . . . but you go on doing it. You can't work out what the problem is, where it's coming from, so you don't know how to stop it.

Pause.

Anna   I'm going to get the desk and drag it out here and destroy it.

Bill   Anna – (*Stops.*) . . . I didn't mean to.

Anna   It leaked into all of us, what Albert did.

Bill   I'll go and fetch the desk. I need to empty some things out of the drawer before we smash it to smithereens.

Anna   Call me if you need a hand.

Anna *swings the axe into the door.* **Bill** *goes into the house.* **Jack** *walks into the garden. He wears an old tee shirt and combats.*

Jack   I thought I'd find you here.

– Don't be frightened.

Anna   I'm not frightened.

Bill *comes back, having heard* **Jack**.

Bill   Did I invite you into my garden?

Jack   I came to see Anna.

Bill   And does she want to see you?

Jack   Does she have to ask your permission?

You're her minder, are you?

Bill   I can see why you lost your job.

Jack   I didn't lose it, I walked out. Had a disagreement with the Head Ranger about the way they do things.

Bill   That's an interesting version of what he told me.

Anna   Dad –

Bill   – What?

Anna   I can chop this up on my own.

Bill   I'll be in the house . . .

He exits into the house.

Jack   Must be nice to have such a protective Dad.

What are you doing? I said what are you doing?

Anna *brandishes the axe.*

Anna   Making fairy cakes.

Jack   . . . I knew you'd come back, Anna.

Anna   The house is full of mud, we need to clear it out.

Jack   I want you to know, I'm prepared to forgive you,
Anna.

(*Pause.*) I'd like to give you another chance.

Even though the way you behaved was unacceptable.
Shouting at me weirdly, hitting me and then running off and
leaving me.

Pause.

Anna   Do you want to talk about what really happened?

Jack (*slight pause*)   I can't trust you.

Anna   That's sad. It's all sad.

Jack   Are you trying to make me hit you?

Anna   Woah!

She puts down the axe.

Jack   I've never got this angry with any woman before.

Anna (*calmly*)   I don't believe you.

Silence.

I made a lot of mistakes.

Jack   Nice to hear you admit it.

Anna   I've spent my whole life trying to work out why things always seemed to be my fault. You pushed me right to the edge . . .

So I went down, to the bottom of it . . . And I understood, finally, that whenever I met a man looking for someone to blame, I was only too willing to be that person, because –

. . . I'll wait till you've finished looking at your fingernails.

Jack   Oh, may I talk now?

Jack *takes something from his pocket and offers it to* **Anna**.

Jack   I found a whitey pebble . . .

Down in the mud, on the shore, there's all sorts of things.

I think it's a finger bone.

Anna   Put it back. It's someone else's memory.

. . . I've had enough of them.

Jack   So what do you think? About getting back together?

Anna   I'd like you to go now, please.

Pause.

Jack   Are you going out with someone else?

Anna   No.

Slight pause.

But I hope to, in a while.

Jack   You want some easy, soft man, don't you . . . Someone who lets you do what you want!

Anna   Will you go now.

Jack   Why?

Anna   Because I'm asking you to go. That's it. That simple.

Go. Please. Now.

Jack *slowly backs away still facing her.*

Jack You'll never heal your pain without me, Anna.

I understood you Anna. No one else will.

Anna *ignores him and picks up the axe.*

Jack *walks away into the open hills.*

Bill *re-enters from the house, carrying a large old biscuit tin.*

Bill He'd better not show his face here again.

Anna Leave it Dad. My business.

Bill You've been a right luggins when it comes to choosing blokes to go out with.

Anna I think that's going to change.

Anna *takes the tin from* **Bill**.

Anna What have you got in here, biscuits?

Bill Oh, this and that from my desk drawer.

Anna *opens the lid of the tin and looks in at the papers.*

Anna The first flyer I did about kids' gardens in schools.

Bill I've got most of your others.

Pause.

There's not much else I want from that house, it all stinks.

Anna Does Mum want anything? – Her clothes are still upstairs.

Bill She wants to move as far away from here as possible. If I even mention I'm coming over here, she walks out of the room.

Slight pause.

I'm sure she'll want to see you in a while . . . only – anyone that reminds her – at the moment – she can't cope.

Slight pause.

Some days she says she's leaving me, only I take no notice and the next day she's asking what I want for tea.

Anna   It wasn't your fault, Dad.

Bill   It felt like that, for thirty years. If the woman who's married you is always unhappy, or unwell. I could never give her a hug without feeling I was doing it wrong.

Slight pause.

Right, I need a hand with the desk, it's at the top of the stairs.

Anna   And I want a sandwich. What have you brought?

Bill   Cheese and pickle.

Anna   Great. I brought mustard and cress, I'm growing it in a pot beside my tent.

Bill   Look at it – our life's work in ruins. (*The house.*)

Anna   Things have to fall apart and be ruined and then we can come up with something better.

Bill   As long as it is better. Next time.

– You'll do that, won't you?

Anna (*slight pause*)   I'll give it a go. I felt like I could never grow up. And now I can.

Lights fade. Sheep call, a curlew calls.

End of play.